Learning to Learn

Student activities for developing work, study and exam-writing skills

MIKE COLES

CHAS WHITE

PIP BROWN

Pembroke Publishers Limited

Pembroke Publishers
538 Hood Road
Markham, Ontario, Canada L3R 3K9
www.pembrokepublishers.com

Distributed in the U.S. by Stenhouse Publishers
477 Congress Street
Portland, ME 04101
www.stenhouse.com

This edition is adapted from *Learning Matters: Active Approaches to Studying*
originally published by Carel Press Ltd. in the United Kingdom in 2000.

The authors would like to recognize the contribution of Les Parsons to the
development work on this edition. Also thank you to the following for their help in
creating this resource: Julian Culley, Ann Daniels, Kate Forrest, Wendy Gilpin, Liz
Hodgkinson, Nick Hunt, Bill Lacey, Neil McAllister, C.R. Macchiusi, Steve Mayes,
Dawn Richards, Chris E. Shepherd, Shirley White and Mike Wilkins.

National Library of Canada Cataloguing in Publication

Coles, Mike
    Learning to learn : student activities for developing work, study, and
exam skills / Mike Coles, Chas White, Pip Brown. — 1st Canadian ed.

Includes bibliographical references and index.
ISBN 1-55138-153-2

    1. Study skills—Study and teaching. 2. Test-taking skills—Study and
teaching. I. White, Chas. II. Brown, Pip III. Title.

LB1049.C64 2003   371.3'028'1   C2002-906052-4

Editor: Christine A. Shepherd, Kathryn Cole
Cover Design: John Zehethofer
Layout Design: MFP Design, Jay Tee Graphics Ltd.
Illustrations: Craig Mitchell

Printed and bound in Canada
9 8 7 6 5 4 3 2

Contents

Introduction   *5*

Unit 1: Managing time and space   *6*

Rate your approach to studying: student questionnaire   *9*
But I don't have time!   *10*
How do you spend your time?   *11*
Evaluating your time management   *12*
Time planning practice   *13*
Planning your time   *14*
Where do you study?   *15*

Unit 2: Note making   *16*

Ineffective note making   *18*
Effective note making   *19*
Rating your notes   *20*
Key words in note making   *21*
Sprays   *22*
Pattern notes   *23*
Abbreviations   *24*

Unit 3: Library and research skills   *25*

Where to look in the library   *28*
Selecting the right book   *30*
A practice search   *31*
Independent study and research projects: Successful assignments   *32*
Computers and research   *35*
Bibliographies and references   *37*

Unit 4: Reading strategies   *38*

Purpose and method   *41*
Skimming   *42*
Scanning   *43*
Reading strategies practice   *44*
SQ3R: A reading strategy for assignments   *47*
Unlocking new vocabulary   *49*
Interpreting data   *50*
Presenting data   *53*
Recommended reading   *54*
Reading list summaries   *56*

Unit 5: Learning   *60*

Understanding memory   *63*
Memory tricks   *64*
Roadblocks to learning   *65*
Concentration and motivation   *66*
Pinpointing your problems   *67*
Achievers and underachievers   *68*
Reflections on learning   *69*

Unit 6: Writing essays   *70*

Planning an essay   *73*
Beginning an essay   *74*
Revising an essay   *77*
Evaluating an essay   *78*
Developing an argument   *79*
Evaluating an argument   *81*
Writing an argument   *83*
Using a thesaurus   *84*
Checklist for essay writing   *87*

Unit 7: Exams   *88*

No surprises   *91*
Writing exams   *92*
Checking the exam paper   *93*
Exam dos and don'ts   *94*
Self-assessment 1: Keeping track   *95*
Self-assessment 2: Progress report   *96*
Handling stress   *97*
Relaxation   *99*

Index   *101*

Introduction

The contrasting abilities of being able to work for a short period of time under pressure, and being able to organize work over a longer period of time, are both vital for students.

To succeed in tests and examinations, students must be able to:

- study effectively giving a suitable amount of time to each subject,
- cope with test and examination nerves,
- interpret the exam paper,
- understand the language of questions,
- recall pertinent points,
- work under pressure to strict time limits,
- check work quickly.

To succeed in research and independent study projects, students need to be able to:

- analyze a topic, project, or question,
- discuss the approach with the teacher,
- research the topic effectively,
- make a plan,
- make a work timetable flexible enough to cope with the unexpected,
- draft their work,
- meet the deadline.

It is important to recognize that no single study method will suit all students. However, students who have had a proper opportunity to experiment with various approaches will be able to more easily develop their own approach, and be more flexible when a task requires several approaches. **Learning to Learn** affords students the opportunity to adapt to and to adopt new, effective skills, and become versed in a variety of approaches to their school responsibilities.

Each of the seven units in this book is preceded by teaching suggestions for the various unit activities. The suggestions include how to introduce or present each activity, the estimated amount of class time required, possible discussion questions, and additional related activities.

All student activity pages are in an easy-to-photocopy format.

Unit 1

Managing time and space

Most students have the best of intentions: they want to do well in school, get good grades, and improve each term. Young people also live egocentric, emotional, and subjective lives. Their best of intentions often get lost in a jumble of competing priorities, crises, and deadlines. They need help to reflect objectively on how they manage their time and their work and study routines; they also need practical strategies to become more efficient and effective in their approach to their school responsibilities.

Activity:
"Rate your approach to studying: student questionnaire"
pg. 9   (40 min.)

Purpose:
To help students analyze and reflect on their present work and study habits.

Reassure the students that the results of the questionnaire are for their information only. When they finish, they will be able to mark their own papers with an answer key you will provide. If they answer frankly and honestly, the questionnaire will give them some practical ideas for improving their work and study habits. After they mark their questionnaires, use the discussion questions below to help them focus on the results.

Answer Key:

	1	2	3	4	5	6	7	8	9	10	11	12	13	14	15	16	17	18	19	20	21	22	23	24	25
A	2	3	2	2	1	2	3	2	1	1	2	2	2	2	2	2	2	2	1	1	2	2	1	3
B	1	1	1	2	1	2	1	2	3	3	3	1	1	1	1	1	1	2	1	1	2	3	3	3	0	1
C	3	1	3	3	3	3	1	1	1	1	3	3	3	3	3	3	0	3	2	3	0	0	0	3	0

Discussion questions

What do you think: a "3" indicates on the questionnaire? Give an example.
a "0" indicates? Give an example.
a "2" or a "1" might mean? Give examples.

Additional activity: Instruct the students to develop three lists from the questionnaire noting: excellent work and study habits, habits that require some adjustment, and habits that require major adjustment.

Activity:
"But I don't have time!"
pg. 10   (40 min.)

Purpose:
To help students set practical goals.

Explain that when many students set goals for their schoolwork they tend to think in generalities. After a report card, for example, students will promise to work harder, study more, do their homework, or pay more attention in class. Although their intentions are sincere, nothing seems to change. This activity is designed to help them focus on specific, attainable approaches to improvement. After discussing the results, use the additional activity to personalize the reflections.

Discussion questions

What problems had the most solutions? What were the solutions?
What solutions seemed too general? How could you make them more specific?
How could you measure whether or not you've acted on a problem?

Additional activity: Instruct students to choose two problems that apply to them personally. For each of those problems, they should devise as many practical, measurable solutions as they can. Advise them to consider how and when they would assess the success of the solutions.

Activity:
"How do you spend your time?" pg. 11 (40 min.)

Purpose:
To help students objectively map out their use of time.

Most students are unaware of how they use time. Like most of us, they often believe that they will achieve more than they do. Unless they can get a clear, objective picture of how they actually spend their time, they won't be able to reorganize how they go about dealing with their schoolwork responsibilities. Again, emphasize that this activity is not a test. Its only purpose is to help them cope with the demands on their time. The discussion questions serve as a way to introduce the activity.

Discussion questions

How do you decide how much time to put toward your schoolwork?
How often and why do you feel that there just aren't enough hours in the day?
When you are planning your time, what factors help you decide to do or not do something?

Additional activity: What time of day is busiest and/or most stressful for you? What kinds of things are you usually doing at that time? How do you feel? What time of day is your most restful and enjoyable? Why?

Activity:
"Evaluating your time management" pg. 12 (40 min.)

Purpose:
To help students analyze and reflect on their use of time.

This activity is a direct follow-up to the previous activity, "How do you spend your time?" With the planner of how they now spend their time in front of them, instruct students to complete the evaluation sheet. The discussion questions are meant to expand on and extend their reflections.

Discussion questions

Did anything surprise you about your use of time? What?
What aspect of your time management do you need to change? Why?
What connections can you make between your use of time and specific, problematic school tasks?

Additional activity: Imagine that exam time is creeping up on you. You know that you need to study. Make a list of your subjects and estimate a mark for each that you feel is a fair indication of what you might receive if the exam were held today. Now estimate how much time you would have to devote to each subject over a two-week period to improve that mark. Where would that time come from?

Activity:

"Time planning practice"
pg. 13   (15 min.)

"Planning your time"   pg. 14
(40 min.)

Purpose:

To help students apply what they've learned about time management.

With these two activities, students first plan in a generic way and then focus specifically on their personal time management. When they begin the "Planning your time" activity, they should have the recent activity, "How do you spend your time?", in front of them to assist with filling in both commitments and priorities.

Discussion questions

What did you find most difficult to plan? Why?

What part of your life don't you have enough time for? Can you do anything about it?

How are you going to make yourself follow your new plan?

Additional activity: Look at the plan you've created for next week. Place check marks on any changes to the way you normally spend your time. Place a question mark on any of the check marks you think might be difficult to implement. Add to the last day of your planner the task of reviewing how well you were able to deal with those changes.

Activity:

"Where do you study?"
pg. 15   (40 min.)

Purpose:

To help students evaluate their home study environment.

Where a student studies can have a significant impact on how well the studying is accomplished. Sometimes, of course, students have few options. This activity is designed to help students reflect on what their conscious or unconscious decisions have been in regard to their home study environment and to justify those decisions. A good way to introduce the topic is with the discussion questions. Before initiating the discussion, survey how many students listen to music as they study and the kind of music they listen to. Inquire, as well, how many do their homework in front of the TV. As the discussion proceeds, however, be wary of absolutes. Many students work with music in the background; if it's not too loud or obtrusive, the music may act as a barrier between the student and various distractions and actually aid concentration.

Discussion questions

How does listening to music as you study or do homework affect your concentration?

How does watching television as you study or do homework affect your concentration?

What difference, if any, would a particular room, chair, or table or desk make to your ability to concentrate?

Additional activity: Ask students to review the various activities in this unit and make a list of those points about managing their time and space that will make the most difference to their individual situations.

Rate your approach to studying

Student Questionnaire

(Please circle your answers)

1. Do you find it difficult to get down to doing your homework or studying?   A. Sometimes   B. Always   C. Never

2. Do you do most of your schoolwork: A. before 9 p.m.?   B. after 9 p.m.?   C. before school?

3. Do you study without taking breaks?   A. Sometimes   B. Always   C. Never

4. Do you put off homework and studying until the last minute?   A. Sometimes   B. Always   C. Never

5. How far ahead do you plan your studying?   A. Don't plan ahead   B. 1–2 days   C. 3 or more days in advance

6. Do you study with music or the TV on?   A. Sometimes   B. Always   C. Never

7. Do you study: A. in the same place all the time?   B. in a couple of places?   C. anywhere you can find?

8. Do you always have what you need with you? (e.g., textbooks, assignments, notebooks, pens)   A. Sometimes   B. Always   C. Never

9. Do you work on: A. your knee?   B. a table or desk?   C. the floor?

10. Do you work in good lighting?   A. Sometimes   B. Always   C. Never

11. Do you find it difficult to concentrate?   A. Sometimes   B. Always   C. Never

12. Are you interrupted a lot (phone, friends, family)?   A. Sometimes   B. Always   C. Never

13. Do outside interests (clubs, sports, TV, other activities) leave you little time for schoolwork?   A. Sometimes   B. Always   C. Never

14. Do you have trouble understanding assignments?   A. Sometimes   B. Always   C. Never

15. Do you read quite slowly?   A. Sometimes   B. Always   C. Never

16. Do you spend so much time on a few subjects that you don't have time for others?   A. Sometimes   B. Always   C. Never

17. Do you worry about your schoolwork?   A. Only at exam time   B. All the time   C. Never

18. Do you find it difficult to remember things?   A. Sometimes   B. Always   C. Never

19. At the end of the week do you close your books and forget about them until Monday?   A. Sometimes   B. Always   C. Never

20. Can you find what you need in the library?   A. If the librarian helps   B. Yes, but it's difficult   C. Usually I have no trouble

21. Do you understand your notes when studying?   A. Sometimes   B. Always   C. Never

22. Do you find essays easy to write?   A. Sometimes   B. Always   C. Never

23. Do you think your exam results reflect the effort you put into studying?   A. Sometimes   B. Always   C. Never

24. Are you making progress in your subjects?   A. Some of them   B. None of them   C. All of them

25. Do you plan a piece of work before you write it?   A. Sometimes   B. Always   C. Never

But I don't have time!

Have you ever said:

> I can't do it!
> I'm busier than other people.
> I haven't got time to plan.
> I'm too busy to be organized.

Select three problems that fit you, then find possible solutions — you may find more than one for each problem! Match the letter of the problem with the appropriate numbers of the solutions.

Problems

A. I keep getting interrupted.
B. I'm always in a rush and I just seem to leave things to the last minute.
C. I can't concentrate.
D. I keep putting things off.
E. I want to get going, but I've got so much to do I don't know where to start.
F. I start lots of things but I can't seem to finish them.
G. If a piece of work begins to drag on I get tired of it.
H. If I've left something for a week or so, I seem to lose the thread. Sometimes I can't find the work I did, or I can't work out where I'm up to.

Possible solutions

1. Decide on priorities for yourself. Make a list of tasks then write beside each:
    Urgent
    Important
    Can wait
2. Look at how you are spending your time now. Compare this with your priorities.
3. Spend five minutes each evening planning your next day's work. This allows you to sleep on things and saves time in the morning.
4. For most people the morning is the best time to work. Plan your leisure activities at other times. It's said that 80% of your real work is done in 20% of your time.
5. Make a planning system that works for you.
6. Decide what you need to do then do it.
7. Most people want to do their work to the highest possible standard, but you can't always achieve perfection.
8. If you can, do one task at a time. You could start with the most important or the quickest. You'll feel a lot better for finishing something.
9. Vague ambitions won't get you far. Set some definite goals. These will stop your ambitions from simply being daydreams. Clear goals give you confidence and a sense of direction.
10. Make realistic and achievable goals. You should be able to measure how close you are getting to achieving them.
11. Find somewhere quiet to work. Tell people you're going to do some work now, but will see them at such and such a time.
12. Set deadlines.
13. Work in short bursts and plan breaks so you don't have to concentrate for long periods.

How do you spend your time?

Do you have trouble getting down to work?
Do you rush your work to meet deadlines?
Are your study sessions as effective as you'd like?

A planner will help you to meet your study targets. First you must look at how you spend your time **now**. Fill in the planner below as accurately as possible. Leave out school lessons, but do put in:

Private study and homework
Activities and commitments: e.g., sports, reading, household jobs, TV programs, clubs, hobbies
Free time

Color code your chart like this:

Red — Study, homework
Blue — Activities and commitments
Black — Free time

STUDY WEEK PLANNER 1   How you spend your time now

	7–9a.m.	9–11a.m.	11–1p.m.	1–3p.m.	3–5p.m.	5–7p.m.	6–9p.m.	9–10p.m.
S A T								
S U N								

	7–9a.m.	9–3p.m.	3–5p.m.	5–7p.m.	7–9p.m.	9–10p.m.
M O N		LESSONS				
T U E						
W E D						
T H U						
F R I						

Evaluating your time management

Now that you can see how you spend your time, please complete this table.

	Hours, minutes a week
Study/homework	
Activities and commitments	
Free time	

Are you making the best use of your time?

Things I didn't have time for

_____

_____

_____

How much time did I waste? On what?

_____

_____

_____

_____

A study timetable

1. Gives you a target to aim for

2. Spreads your study throughout the week

3. Saves time in decision making, and lets you get down to things

4. Helps you to establish a routine for study

5. Encourages you to keep up with your work.

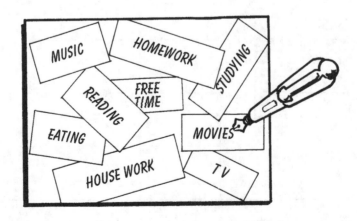

Time planning practice

Plan Claire's evening

- Claire has a chapter of a history book to read: 45 minutes

- a science problem: 30 minutes

- an English assignment: 30 minutes

- Claire wants to phone her boyfriend: 15 minutes

- see two TV programs, 6:30–7:00, 9:30–10:30

- do her fitness training: between 30 minutes and an hour.

Dinner is over by 6:00 p.m. Her parents like her to be in bed by 11:00 p.m. Divide up Claire's evening so that she can do all these things.

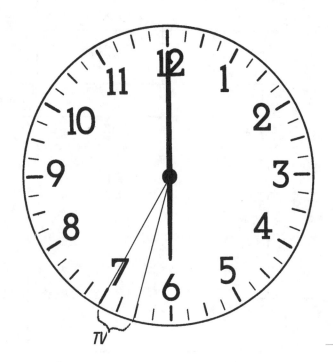

Check off these points as you prepare to work on the next activity, *Planning your time*.

1. Note things that you must do. ❑

2. Plan at least 8 hours study/homework over 7 days (12–15 hours at exam time) ❑

3. Study periods of less than 10 minutes aren't of much use. ❑

4. Planned breaks are essential to successful study. You should not study for more than 45 minutes without a 5 minute break. ❑

5. You study best when you feel fresh. Avoid late hours. Working late makes you a tired learner. ❑

Planning your time

STUDY WEEK PLANNER 2 The future

Mark in first on this planner your permanent commitments. If you are unsure what to add next, make a list of tasks so that you can work out in what order to do things.

	7–9a.m.	9–11a.m.	11–1p.m.	1–3p.m.	3–5p.m.	5–7p.m.	7–9p.m.	9–10p.m.
S A T								
S U N								

	7–9a.m.	9–3p.m.	3–5p.m.	5–7p.m.	7–9p.m.	9–10p.m.
M O N		LESSONS				
T U E						
W E D						
T H U						
F R I						

If you persevere in making a weekly planner you will soon establish the habits of:

❏ planning ahead,

❏ using your time effectively,

and these will become part of your approach to study.

After just a few weeks you will know your best times for study. You can then reserve these times for your most important work.

Where do you study?

1. In what room do you usually study or do your homework?

   _____

2. If you sit, what kind of chair do you use? If you don't sit, describe your position.

   _____

   _____

3. What do you use as a desk?

   _____

   _____

4. When do you usually study or do your homework (days of the week and hours of the day)?

   _____

   _____

   _____

5. List what you think are the four most important qualities of a good study place. Put them in order of importance.

   A. _____

   B. _____

   C. _____

   D. _____

6. Write down four changes you would like to make to your place of study.

   A. _____

   _____

   B. _____

   _____

   C. _____

   _____

   D. _____

   _____

Unit 2

Note making

Thinking and language are so closely linked that for all intents and purposes they're two sides to the same coin. As with the other language strands, we also think through writing. When students write to understand, as opposed to copying to aid rote memorization, they are involved in a high-level thinking activity that enhances and deepens learning. Note making as an approach to learning has a number of facets that benefit from direct teaching and practice.

Activity:
"Ineffective note making"
pg. 18   (20 min.)

"Effective note making"
pg. 19   (20 min.)

Purpose:
To help students analyze and compare samples of effective and ineffective note making.

These two activities should be completed during the same time period. Introduce the activities by placing the following true or false questions on the chalk board:

Note making is a dull and difficult experience: true or false?
Notes that use the language of text books are hard to understand: true or false?
Note making is a waste of time: true or false?

In the discussion that ensues, you should be able to centre in on the reasons for taking notes and the reasons why note making is often so difficult. The activities emphasize how effective note-making skills can enhance learning. The discussion questions can be used to sum up the activities.

Discussion questions

What prevents people from always writing effective notes?
What are some solutions for these problems?

Additional activity: Instruct students to bring two of their notebooks to class next day; science and history or geography notebooks would be best. These notebooks will be used in the next day's activities.

Activity:
"Rating your notes"
pg. 20   (40 min.)

Purpose:
To help students evaluate their note making and set goals for improvement.

Students should have with them their own science and history or geography notebooks. The first part of the activity reviews some of the points made in the "Effective note making" activity. Begin by discussing some of the techniques not covered in that exercise, such as use of color coding or highlighting. The discussion questions focus on setting specific, attainable goals.

Discussion questions

What kind of practical, attainable goals could you set for improving your note-making skills?
When you set a note-making goal, how can you measure whether or not you've attained that goal?

Additional activity: Instruct the students to choose a note from one of their notebooks that could be improved. Ask them to make a list of all the features they would change if they had the opportunity. Make sure you let them know that they won't actually have to make those changes so that the suggestions are more forthcoming.

Activity:

"Key words in note making" pg. 21   (40 min.)

Purpose:

To help students understand and learn to use key words when making notes.

Introduce the concept with the five reasons for note making found at the top of the activity sheet. Instruct the students to underline the key words in each point. Review the results and continue on with the main activity based on the Hawaiian Monarchy passage. The discussion questions can be used after a few students have read their final note.

Discussion questions

What difficulties do you encounter when someone asks you to write a note in your own words?
Should everyone find the same key words? Why or why not?
What is the most difficult kind of note to make? Why?

Additional activity: Try using the key words approach with the next note you are asked to make in any subject area. Be prepared to report back on how it worked out.

Activity:

"Sprays" pg. 22   (20 min.)

"Pattern notes" pg. 23 (40 min.)

Purpose:

To introduce students to alternative ways of making notes.

Begin the lesson with the phrase, "note making," on the chalk board. Ask the students for points that come to mind about note making that have already been discussed in previous classes. As the ideas unfold, construct a sample "spray" note on the chalk board. Direct them next to the sample "spray" and "pattern" notes on the activity sheets and use the discussion questions below to investigate the two forms before assigning the activities.

Discussion questions

What kind of note making or subject area would suit a "spray?" Why?
What kind of note making or subject area would suit a "pattern?" Why?

Additional activity: Exchange the "spray" and "pattern" notes you've created with someone else in class. Notice the similarities and differences. Identify ideas you might like to use yourself next time you attempt one of these forms.

Activity:

"Abbreviations" pg. 24 (40 min.)

Purpose:

To help students learn about and apply the use of abbreviations in their note making.

Begin with the phrase, "Hw r u?" on the chalk board. Students will be familiar with this kind of abbreviation from using e-mail. Ask for other common abbreviations used online and write them on the chalk board. Just as this kind of writing saves time and effort online, other abbreviations can serve the same purposes with note making.

Discussion questions

What problems, if any, can you foresee with using abbreviations?
Why isn't the abbreviated language of computer chat rooms and e-mail used elsewhere in newspapers and text books?

Additional activity: Choose a short passage from one of your English texts and rewrite it using as many abbreviations, symbols, and computer language shortcuts as you can. Ask someone else to read the new passage and see how much difficulty they encounter, if any.

Ineffective note making

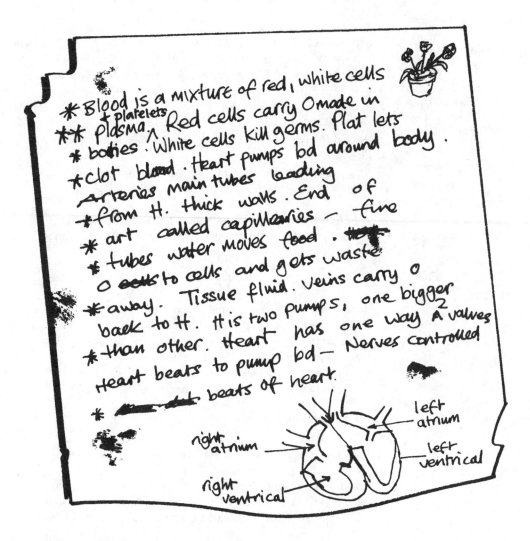

1. Using a colored pen, circle and underline all of the features of the note above that could be improved.

2. Make a list of these weak features you've discovered.

_____

_____

_____

_____

_____

_____

Effective note making

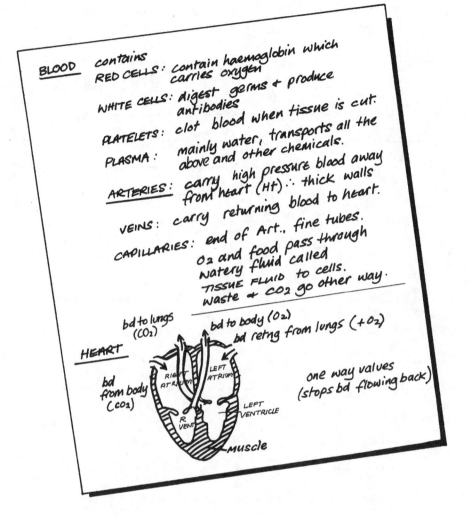

1. Using a colored pen, check off all of the strong features you can find on the notes above.

2. Make a list of these strong features you've discovered.

_____

_____

_____

_____

_____

_____

_____

Rating your notes

A. List 10 features an ideal set of notes would have, such as complete table of contents or neat handwriting. An ideal notebook would have:

    1. _____

    2. _____

    3. _____

    4. _____

    5. _____

    6. _____

    7. _____

    8. _____

    9. _____

    10. _____

B. List up to five features of your notes you think are good to excellent.

    1. _____

    2. _____

    3. _____

    4. _____

    5. _____

C. List up to five features of your notes you think you could improve.

    1. _____

    2. _____

    3. _____

    4. _____

    5. _____

D. Choose the one feature of your notes you would like to improve most. Use it to complete the following note-making goal:

For the next week, I am going to _____

_____

_____

Key words in note making

We make notes to help us:

❑ concentrate on learning,

❑ put ideas into our own words and diagrams,

❑ link new knowledge to what we already know,

❑ identify the main points and supporting details,

❑ remember.

One essential skill in note making is finding the key words in a passage. Key words are the ones most loaded with meaning, the ones that encourage memory.

1. As you read the following passage, underline the key words that help you trace the important steps in the creation and then the abolishment of the Hawaiian monarchy.

2. Make a list of the key words you've underlined.

3. Replace as many of the key words as you can with words you would normally use, or with synonyms.

4. Using your revised key words, write a shortened note with a new title that accurately reflects the main ideas.

The Hawaiian Monarchy

Honolulu's stately Iolani Palace is the only true royal manor in the United States, but then, **Hawaii** is the only state that was once a kingdom with its own monarchy. When Captain James Cook came to the Hawaiian Islands in 1778, he introduced cannons and other western arms. Between 1790 and 1791, the warrior king, Kamehameha, used these weapons to unite the Hawaiian Islands into one kingdom. According to Hawaiian legend, Kamehameha was also assisted by the fire goddess, Pele, who rained burning lava on the heads of the king's enemies.

Having established the Kingdom of **Hawaii**, Kamehameha the Great became the first of a dynasty that would rule **Hawaii** for more than a century. During this time, the monarchy's power gradually diminished, as growing numbers of American missionaries and businessmen came to own much of **Hawaii**'s land. In 1893, a group of American businessmen, aided by U.S. Marines, overthrew the last of the monarchs, Queen Liliuokalani, and imprisoned her in Iolani Palace.

The queen's heir, Princess Kaiulani, travelled to Washington to seek the help of President Grover Cleveland. Cleveland condemned the monarchy's overthrow after learning it had been done against the will of the Hawaiian people. His sentiments were not shared by the next president, William McKinley, who officially annexed **Hawaii** into the United States. **Hawaii** became a state in 1959.

In 1993, the U.S. Congress and President Bill Clinton formally apologized on behalf of the government for the overthrow of the Hawaiian monarchy. Since then, some native Hawaiians have petitioned for the right to restore their monarchy and regain control of their land.

Grolier Encyclopedia, Lands and Peoples Online, Grolier Pub. Co. Inc., 2003

Sprays

Sprays are a way of quickly jotting down all your ideas on a subject and linking them up. Sprays save time because you don't have to write sentences or put words down in any particular order.

Stage 1: Putting the words down as they occur to you

Stage 2: Making the links

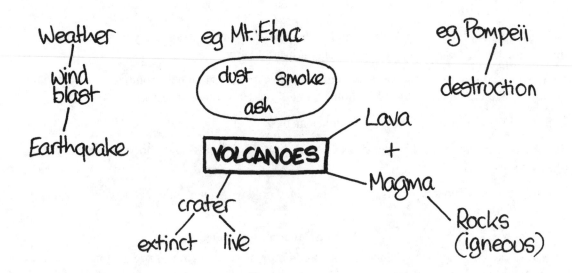

Now make a spray about a topic you are studying.

Pattern notes

If you want to keep your notes and use them later you need to organize them. Pattern notes are a very effective way of planning an essay or of preparing a summary of a section of work. They are an absorbing and fruitful method of reviewing. This pattern note on first aid was made by a pupil after an introductory talk. Notice her use of space, shape, lettering, keywords, grouping and the way she has linked ideas together. Use color to make this pattern note clearer. Now make your own pattern note on a subject you are studying.

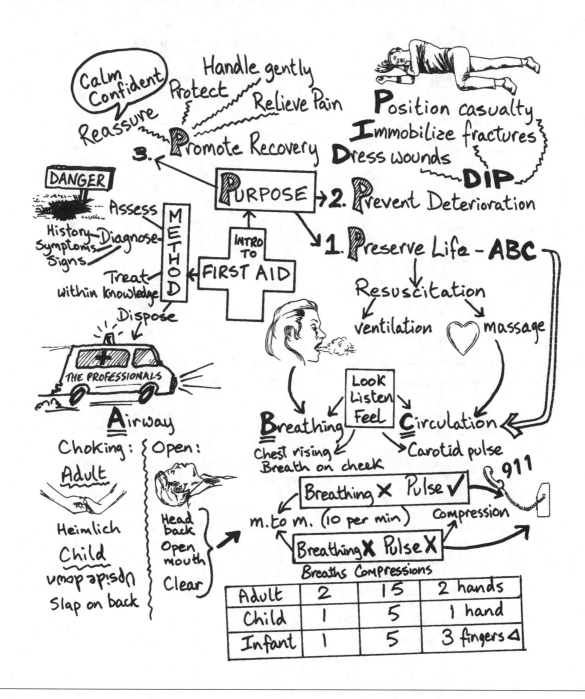

Abbreviations

❏ Abbreviations (Abvs) save time and space when writing notes.

❏ Some books have a list of abbreviations at the front.

❏ Some students write notes with connecting words missing. Saves time + space, be careful when reading notes, interpret accurately.

❏ You could leave out the vowels of common words, as long as the meaning remains clear, for example gd, hlp, grps.

❏ Record any abbreviations of your own that you are going to use at the front of your file.

1. Note down the meaning of the following abbreviations and symbols.

= _____	@ _____	♂ _____
% _____	× _____	ie _____
− _____	∴ _____	_____
$ _____	NB _____	_____
∴ _____	eg _____	_____
♀ _____	Kg _____	_____
cm _____	+ _____	_____
≠ _____	& _____	_____

2. Add some of your own abbreviations.

3. Read this passage about the foundation of the Red Cross. Notes have been made about the first paragraph. Make notes about the rest of the passage to practise using abbreviations.

In 1859 a Swiss businessman, Henri Dunant, was so horrified by the suffering of wounded troops at the battle of Solferino that he organized volunteer groups of local villagers to help them.

In 1862 Dunant wrote *A Memory of Solferino* which called for permanent societies to care for war wounded and argued for the protection of both medical services and the wounded. This inspired the foundation of the Red Cross movement in Switzerland in October 1863.

The Geneva Convention of 1864 was an international agreement to adopt both these ideals and the Red Cross as a symbol of care for the injured and protection from attack.

The Red Cross is not a Christian symbol. It is, in fact, an inversion of the Swiss national flag (which is a white cross on a red background). Nevertheless, in Muslim countries the Red Crescent is preferred as an emblem.

1859   Battle of <u>Solferino</u> shocked Henri <u>Dunant</u>
∴ organized vlteers to hlp.

Unit 3

Library and research skills

With the advent of the Internet and the transformation of libraries into multimedia resource centers, teachers are placing more and more emphasis in their programs on independent research projects. Students not only need sophisticated skills to access information from a variety of sources, but they also need to discriminate among those sources. Among the books, online encyclopedias, CDs, and the Internet, they have to decide where and how they can most efficiently find solutions for their specific problems.

Activity:

"Where to look in the library" pg. 28   (40 min.)

Purpose:

To provide students with the practical background necessary to efficiently use the library.

Write on the chalk board, "Now that we have the Internet and CD-ROMs, why do we need libraries?" Solicit and list opinions from the class. Inquire about practical problems students have encountered when using the library.

Discussion questions

Which questions were the most difficult to match with classification numbers? Why?

If you walked into the library with a topic and didn't know the appropriate classification number, what could you do?

What is the difference between the way a school library and a public library are arranged?

Additional activity: Before the next class, choose one of your own questions from the "Where would you find . . .?" activity, visit the library, and write down the titles of five books in which you might expect to find the answers.

Activity:

"Selecting the right book" pg. 30   (20 min.)

Purpose:

To offer students engaged in research, criteria for discriminating among similar, non-fiction books.

Prepare for the lesson by obtaining four or five non-fiction books on the same subject from the library. Place them in full view of the class. Ask the students what they would do if they were looking for information on a particular topic and came across these five books; how would they decide which ones to use? Use the discussion questions to examine the practical problems involved in trying to find "the right book."

Discussion questions

What are the major problems someone might encounter when trying to find information in a book?

What kind of information can you obtain from an index that you might not get from a table of contents?

Additional activity: Choose two of your non-fiction text books. Compare date of publication, reading level, number and quality of illustrations, size of type, and index. Which is the better book and why?

Activity:
"A practice search"
pg. 31   (40 min.)

Purpose:
To allow students to experience directly what they've learned about choosing books for research.

Reserve a period in your school library for this activity. Instruct the students to choose a topic they would like to research and write it on the activity sheet. Review the assignment and let the students complete it as they explore the library resources. The discussion questions can be used just before the end of the period to sum up the experience.

Discussion questions

What problems, if any, did you encounter as you explored your topic?
How often, when you had problems, were you able to get assistance from someone else in class?
What kinds of questions require the assistance of a teacher or librarian?

Additional activity: For the next activity, students will need an actual independent study or research project. You will need to plan this activity in conjunction with an assignment of your own or in collaboration with a colleague who has such an assignment pending. Prior to employing the next activity, instruct students to come to class with their topic ready.

Activity:
"Independent study and research projects: Successful assignments"
pg. 32   (40 min. introduction)

Purpose:
To give students an opportunity to apply what they've learned about library and research skills by completing an actual independent study or research project.

You will need to plan this activity in conjunction with an independent study or research assignment of your own or in collaboration with a colleague who has such an assignment pending. The introduction to this activity will take one class period. Students will be expected to complete the actual independent or research project, however, within the specific timelines you establish. These sheets provide students with a structure for guiding each stage of the research. As you review the advice in these sheets with your students, tailor the instructions to match your own expectations and objectives. The discussion questions review and emphasize the specific instructions you've given.

Discussion questions

What deadlines should you set for each stage of the project?
How are you going to plan the project?
At what stages must your progress be reviewed with the teacher?

Additional activity: On the day the projects are handed in, review the activity sheets and try to identify the most problematic aspects of the research steps. Offer solutions before the next project arises.

Activity:
"Computers and research"
pg. 35   (40 min.)

Purpose:
To instruct students in the advantages and disadvantages of using the computer for research.

The computer is a double-edged sword. While it offers an incredible amount of information on the Internet, the information is extremely difficult to manage. Teachers often assume that students know more about surfing the web than they actually do: students display an impressive dexterity as they "point and click," but much of what they do is impulsive and counterproductive. The points made on the student activity sheet can help students reflect on and assess their attitudes towards, and facility with, computer research. In discussion, inquire about the validity of each point and possible solutions for relevant problems.

Discussion questions

How valid are the assertions about computer research and the kinds of problems outlined?
What other problems have you encountered?

Additional activity: After your next research session on a computer, review the list of problems and check off the problems you encountered. Also check off the solutions you attempted. What goals can you set for your next session?

Activity:
"Bibliographies and references"
pg. 37   (20 min.)

Purpose:
To provide students with a practical guide for completing bibliographies.

Bibliographies are difficult to write. Students need a style guide on which to model their bibliographies. This sheet is meant as a handy reference. Students should file it in their binders wherever they keep their writing and have it handy when completing research projects. Discuss the various points with the class and insist on the correct usage for their next project.

Where to look in the library

Understanding the Dewey Classification Codes

Each subject is given a code which is put on the spine of the book.

Books can be arranged by this number on the shelf.

To find information on a *topic* you must first find the code number for that subject. Most libraries have their catalogues on computer but you may also find a wall chart or a card catalogue. If there is nothing on your subject, it might be listed under a different name. Try thinking of words which mean the same or almost the same. For example, if you can't find anything under "cheese" in the subject index you could look under "dairy products".

If you know the *author* of the book you want, look up the surname in the author catalogue to get the code.

If you only know the *title* of the book, then ask.

Cracking the code

There are ten main divisions to the code numbers. Each main division is then divided into ten major headings, for example the Pure sciences — the 500s — are divided up in the table below. Each one of these major headings is then divided into ten important subjects, for example Physics, 530, is divided up below.

MAIN DIVISIONS		PURE SCIENCES		PHYSICS	
000	General topics	500	Pure sciences	530	Physics
100	Philosophy & Psychology	510	Mathematics	531	Mechanics
200	Religion	520	Astronomy	532	Mechanics of fluids
300	Society	530	Physics	533	Mechanics of gases
400	Languages	540	Chemistry	534	Sound
500	Pure sciences	550	Geology	535	Light
600	Technology	560	Fossils	536	Heat
700	The arts	570	Biology	537	Electricity & Electronics
800	Literature	580	Botany	538	Magnetism
900	Geography & History	590	Zoology	539	Modern physics

Below are some of the most important codes (librarians call them "classification numbers") for exam subjects. These codes are used in both school and public libraries. Dictionaries and encyclopedias will be kept in the reference section.

Art history	709	History	909
Business studies	650	of the ancient world	930
English literature	820	of Europe	940
English drama	821	of England	942
English novel	823	of Asia	950
English poetry	822	of Africa	960
Food	641	of North America	970
French language	440	of South America	980
French literature	840	Music	780
Geography	910	Sociology	301
of Europe	914	Technology	600
of Asia	915		
of Africa	916		
of North America	917		
of South America	918		

Where would you find . . ?

For the following questions, indicate where in the library you would expect to find the pertinent information by placing the appropriate classification numbers in the box provided. If you find both a general and a more specific number, give the specific number.

1. What's the majority religion in India? ☐

2. What are "black holes?" ☐

3. Where can I find a French grammar book? ☐

4. Were the United States and Canada ever at war? ☐

5. What makes lightning? ☐

6. Who were the Druids? ☐

7. What's the smallest country in South America? ☐

8. How old was the poet, Lord Byron, when he died? ☐

9. What's an aria? ☐

10. What was the first computer like? ☐

11. In what style did Monet paint? ☐

12. How does magnetism work? ☐

13. When did Socrates live? ☐

14. Can you turn a gas into a solid? ☐

15. Where's the best place to find Tyrannosaurus bones? ☐

16. Which mushrooms are poisonous? ☐

17. What's the German author, Goethe, famous for? ☐

18. What's the theory of supply and demand? ☐

Now include four questions of your own on topics of your own choosing and indicate where in the library you would look for the answers:

1. _____ ☐

2. _____ ☐

3. _____ ☐

4. _____ ☐

Selecting the right book

Selecting the right book means rejecting ones that aren't going to be of any use to you. You don't need to begin reading a book at page 1 to find out if it has the information you are seeking. Use the clues in the diagram above to do this quickly.

❏ Make sure the book is not too difficult for you; if the first page has more than five words you do not understand then it probably is.

❏ If you need up-to-date information, then check the book's date of publication — you'll often find this on the page opposite the Contents page.

❏ See if the book has a summary at the end of each chapter or a conclusion at the end of the book. These can save you time. If there is no summary, read the first and last paragraph for each relevant chapter to help you decide if you will need to use it.

Where would you look to see if a book:

1. Had an illustration you wanted? _____

2. Had a qualified author you could quote? _____

3. Was up-to-date? _____

4. Had general information on your topic? _____

5. Had a particular piece of information you were seeking? (e.g. the name of an inventor) _____

6. Was at the right level for you to use? (e.g. not too difficult, or too easy)_____

_____

A practice search

What topic have you chosen to research? _____

What is the classification number for your topic? _____

Find and list five titles on this topic in the library:

1. _____
2. _____
3. _____
4. _____
5. _____

Skim these books looking at the following features: the covers, tables of contents, opening and closing paragraphs of several chapters, illustrations, and indexes.

How are these books similar in their treatment of the topic?

_____

_____

How are they different?

_____

_____

List five questions about your topic that you can answer from these books.

1. _____
2. _____
3. _____
4. _____
5. _____

Choose one and research the answer.

What is the answer to your question?

_____

_____

In what book did you find the answer? _____

When was the book written? _____

On what page did you find the answer? _____

Independent study and research projects: Successful assignments

Follow this guide carefully to make sure you produce your best work as well as save yourself time.

What is my topic?

Write down your topic. If you're not completely certain what this topic means or what exactly you'll need to do, ask your teacher for assistance. If you have any uncertainty at the beginning, that confusion will only grow as you get deeper into your assignment.

What is the deadline for the assignment?

Don't aim to finish on the deadline. This leaves you with no flexibility. Unless you are very well organized and motivated, things can go wrong! Delays creep in or you may put off starting the work. As a result you hand in a very rushed, last minute piece of work, or your work is late. Be realistic — how well have you kept to deadlines in the past? Aim to finish a day or two early.

What happens if I hand in work late?

Late work may not be accepted. If you are late with one piece of work it puts you behind with your other work, and may make you late starting the next piece. This can quickly become a vicious circle — it's depressing, and means that you don't produce good work.

How can I make sure I hand it in on time?

Aim to complete the assignment before the deadline. The more important the assignment, and the longer you have for it, then the more time you need to allow as a safety buffer before the deadline.

How can I set myself targets?

Decide on a personal deadline in advance of the official one. You need to be realistic when you ask yourself, "How long will it take to do these things?"

- ❏ Make a plan.
- ❏ Do the research.
- ❏ Write the rough draft.
- ❏ Revise the rough draft.
- ❏ Produce the final version. If you are using graphs, charts, and illustrations allow extra time.
- ❏ Check the assignment.

What have I got to hand in?

How much and in what form: essay, booklet, chart, cassette or video tape.

Independent study and research projects: Successful assignments — *continued*

How do I make a plan?

Planning is one of the hardest things to do. Many people prefer to plunge straight into the work itself. But a plan will save time in the long run.

There are many different ways to plan. Experiment to see which works best for you. The simplest way is to underline the key words in the title or make a spray diagram of the key ideas. After you have noted the key ideas, number each according to its importance. Keep this plan with you as you start to write. If any new ideas come to you, note them down right away.

When you have completed your plan it would be a good idea to talk it over with your teacher. You also need to check it against the criteria for producing projects. Most courses give some student guidance.

Where can I get the information?

Are all the books and resources you need in the school library? If you're not sure, ask the librarian.

Books: Books you need may be in more than one section of the library. Be sure to check both the lending and reference sections. Think of the key names and terms for your topic and check the Library Subject Index or Decoder Chart for the Dewey Classification codes. For example, if you are writing about nuclear power you could look up these:

Nuclear power or Nuclear energy	621.48
Nuclear industry advertising	659
Power stations	621.4
Nuclear war	355.4
Nuclear disasters	363.179

You'll need to use the contents and index pages fully.

Articles: The librarian may have a collection of newspaper and magazine articles which could be very useful if you need up-to-date information.

Videos, slides, charts, databases, CD-ROMS: Remember to check these sources. If your school library does not have enough material then try the main local public library — it may be best to phone first to see if they can help you.

Specialist organizations: You may need information from organizations. Send a large self-addressed stamped envelope with your letter. It may take some time to get a reply, so you will need to write as soon as possible.

Local organizations: These may be able to help and you might be able to visit them, or interview someone on the phone. The library might have a list of names and addresses. You can also check the phone book and *Yellow Pages*.

Independent study and research projects: Successful assignments — *continued*

How do I select the information?

Keep your key headings in mind. Use the contents pages and indexes of books.

What is the best way to use the information?

You need to make a clear link between what you found and your title and key headings. It is important that the information is in your own words. If you must copy something directly, then put it in quotation marks and say where you've taken the quotation from.

How shall I present it?

Your teacher will probably discuss this with you, and may show you some examples. Remember the saying "One picture is worth a thousand words". Can you use graphs, diagrams, or photographs as well as words to present your findings?

When should I start the first draft?

Start your first draft as soon as possible so that you feel you have a start. If you delay you can quickly lose momentum and interest.

How should I revise the first draft?

Don't start to write up your best version as soon as you've finished the draft. You need time to revise carefully and critically. Your first thoughts are rarely your best.

Check carefully for mistakes. Look for possible improvements, and make sure that you've not left any important points out. Remember to include a list of references if necessary.

Find out if you can discuss this first draft with anyone. It may be possible to discuss it with your teacher.

Should I keep a copy of the assignment?

Yes, on a disc, photocopy, your computer, or at least keep your rough draft.

What does my teacher think of my project?

It's too easy just to concentrate on the grade or mark, but this won't help you to improve for next time. Note your teacher's comment and apply it to your next project.

What do I think of my work now that it has been marked?

Now make your own comment about the assignment. How could you have improved it? Go through this guide again to help you to be critical.

Computers and research

The use of the Internet in school research projects is problematic for a number of reasons:

- It's *one* tool, not the *only* tool.
  - Many students work under the assumption that only the Internet has what they need. They think if they can't use the computer, they can't do research.

- The Internet doesn't have a brain.
  - Many students think the Internet knows more than they do. In their minds, a typographical error in their search request makes no difference; the Internet can figure out what they want; a negative search means no information exists.

- The effective use of the Internet requires the application of a highly sophisticated set of interrelated skills:
  - Many students have no criteria for selecting the appropriate search engine.
  - A simple search often produces a list of hundreds of sites. Students are presented with too many choices and too much information.
  - Many students have difficulty with the concept of a search. They expect the Internet to operate much like an encyclopedia: simply type in your topic and the answer will pop up. They have difficulty narrowing their searches.
  - Few students possess the criteria for deciding on the usefulness of one site over another.
  - Few students possess the background information to evaluate the authenticity and validity of a site.
  - The material is often at an adult reading level.
  - "Point and click" impulses take over from reading and discriminating among the images on the screen. Students seldom read instructions.
  - Non-thinking activities, such as copying and printing pictures and graphics, are a priority.
  - Plagiarism is a constant concern. Students download and print material without change or even without comprehension, and claim it as their own.
  - Many students have difficulty staying on task: too many distractions not related to their search are a "click" away.

Online encyclopedias and CD-ROMs offer an alternative to the Internet with the following advantages:

- Material is organized and categorized; information is easy to find.

- Material is concise; easy to skim and scan for usefulness.

- Reading level is appropriate for full comprehension.

- Information is up-to-date, authentic, and valid.

Computers and research — *continued*

Online encyclopedias and CD-ROMs also possess the following disadvantages:

- Material is often too brief for comprehensive, in-depth treatments.

- Material does not cover up-to-the-moment current events unless augmented by special electronic newspaper and periodical library programs.

Tips for using the Internet:

- Qualify your search as specifically and narrowly as you can; e.g., not "Civil War" but "Civil War Union uniforms".

- Reject any sites that offer a chance to win a prize, or that advertise a service or product.

- Skim the first paragraph; if the material is difficult to understand, leave the site.

- Skim the length of the material; if there's a lot of material and no table of contents or index, leave the site or be prepared to invest a maximum amount of time with no guarantee of success.

- Check the authenticity of the site with the teacher or librarian; better yet, ask the teacher to bookmark recommended sites.

- Stay on task; avoid distractions. If you accidentally log on to an inappropriate site, log off immediately.

- If you haven't answered your question or found some relevant material on a site after about five minutes, consider moving on to another site.

Try this comparison:

Search the Internet and an online encyclopedia with the search word, "eagles". Compare the results using such categories as: number of articles; usefulness of title descriptions; amount of time required to research material; reading level and relevance of material. If you had a specific question about eagles, what would be the best approach to conducting research on the computer? Why?

Bibliographies and references

Bibliographies

Keep this page in your writing binder as a handy reference for all your assignments!

❏ A bibliography is a list of the sources that you have used in the preparation and writing of your project or assignment. (*Biblion* is the Greek word for book; -graphy means a form of writing or representing something, e.g. photography, calligraphy, from the Greek word *graphien* to write.)

❏ A bibliography is an important part of any project. It is the evidence of your research.

❏ A bibliography should be included as a separate sheet, or sheets, at the end of your project.

Each time you consult a source — a book, a journal, a newspaper, a CD-ROM, or a magazine — note the:

❏ Author's surname and initials

❏ Date of publication

❏ Title of the source

❏ Publisher's name

❏ It might be useful to note where you got the book from and, if from a library, the book's classification number.

Bibliographies are written out in alphabetical order.

Bois Y.A. (1999) *Matisse and Picasso*. Flammarion
Picasso P. et al. (2002) *Picasso: 200 Masterpieces from 1898-1972*. Bullfinch Press
Williams E. (1999) *Paris: Walking Tour of the Artist's Life in the City*. Little Bookroom

For journal articles the order is:

White E.A.R. (1992) "Minding your own business," *Journal of Cumbrian Economics*, vol 5 pp321–34.

Underline (or type in italics) titles of books and journals — this makes them easier to spot.

References

References should always state the author's name with the year of publication in brackets.

Adams (1993) suggested that "_____"
or It has been suggested that "_____" Adams (1993)

Quotations must give page numbers.

Adams (1993) states that "the reason why _____" (p. 16)

This allows your teacher to check what you have said, and as importantly, you can find your original source if you need to, saving you hours of searching.

Unit 4

Reading strategies

As students mature, we assume that they have automatically become skilful and fluent readers. Toward the end of the junior grades, as a consequence, many English/Language Arts teachers adjust their main focus from teaching reading to teaching literature. At the same time, the language and concept load in content area texts and reference materials, for example, grow increasingly more sophisticated and complex just as research projects become a priority in most subject areas. Students still require direct teaching of a variety of reading strategies to ensure that their skills are commensurate to the tasks they're assigned.

Activity:

  "Purpose and method"
  pg. 41   (20 min.)

Purpose:

  To help students match how they read with what and why they're reading.

Explain that successful readers vary how they read according to their purpose for reading. Review the five methods as detailed on the student activity sheet and use the discussion questions to explain their application.

Discussion questions

What kind of reading material would you match with each method?
When might you use more than one method with the same material?
For what school subjects might you use one method more than another? Why?

Additional activity: Make a list of the reading experiences you've had over the last few days, such as a novel, a mathematics text, a billboard, or the back of a cereal box. Beside each item, indicate which of the five reading strategies you employed.

Activity:

  "Skimming" pg. 42   (20 min.)

  "Scanning" pg. 43   (20 min.)

Purpose:

  To practise the reading strategies of skimming and scanning.

Many students have the impression that reading means starting at the beginning and working all the way through until you reach the end. Even when you ask them to skim or scan an article, they follow the same pattern. These two activities tell them how to apply the strategies and provide practice for reinforcement. The beginning of each student activity sheet offers a useful introduction to the concepts and the discussion topics extend the concepts into their school tasks.

Discussion questions

When would you skim a magazine or novel?
When would you scan a magazine or novel?
With what kind of school tasks would skimming be helpful?
With what kind of school tasks would scanning be helpful?

Additional activity: The other three reading strategies are: reading for detail, enjoyment, and detecting bias. For each one, indicate several examples from the last week of how you applied, or could have applied, those strategies in your own school work.

Activity:
"Reading strategies practice"
pg. 44 (40 min.)

Purpose:
To practise the various reading strategies on a variety of reading passages.

At this point, students are ready to apply what they've learned about flexible reading strategies. Instruct them to look at the purpose for reading first, decide on the most appropriate reading strategy for the task, and then apply that strategy to the passage. The discussion questions will help them evaluate how flexibly they read.

Discussion questions

What strategy did you use with each passage and why did you choose that strategy?
When were you most uncertain about which strategy to use? Why?
Which strategy do you think is the most difficult to use? Why?

Additional activity: Over the next two days, whenever you have any kind of reading to do for a school-related assignment or activity, note the reading strategy you choose to apply. At the end of that time, look back over the reading tasks and decide which strategies you most used and when a different strategy might have been more successful.

Activity:
"SQ3R: A reading strategy for assignments"
pg. 47 (40 min.)

Purpose:
To learn and apply the reading strategy, SQ3R.

Put the letters, SQRRR, one underneath the other on the chalk board. Tell the students that these letters represent a special reading strategy called "SQ3R" that will help them with many of their school assignments. Complete each letter with the appropriate word and then direct their attention to the explanations at the top of the student activity sheet. The discussion questions and additional activity extend the practice into their actual school assignments.

Discussion questions

With what kind of school assignments would SQ3R be most useful?
How could you ensure that you use the method properly?

Additional activity: As soon as you're given an assignment that might be right for SQ3R, put the words *survey*, *question*, *read*, *review*, and *recall* one underneath the other at the top of a page. As you work your way through the assignment, note beside each word any aspect of each stage you still need to complete. Afterwards, evaluate how effectively you applied the strategy and how useful it's been to you.

Activity:
"Unlocking new vocabulary"
pg. 49 (20 min.)

Purpose:
To practise a strategy for unlocking new vocabulary when reading.

Ask what students do when they encounter a word they don't understand as they're reading. Some of the strategies to validate would be: if the word isn't important to the meaning, skip over it; if the word is important to the meaning, ask a friend or the teacher; use a dictionary. Another strategy would be to examine the prefix or suffix and attempt to guess the meaning. The discussion questions and additional activity extend the assignment.

Discussion questions

What other prefixes not covered in this assignment have you found to be useful?
What other suffixes not covered in this assignment have you found to be useful?

Additional activity: Choose ten examples of words using prefixes and ten examples of words using suffixes from the activity sheet and write a sentence for each. Make sure that the sense of the sentence reinforces or illuminates the meaning of the prefix or suffix.

Activity:
"Interpreting data"
pg. 50 (60 min.)

Purpose:
To help students interpret a variety of charts and graphs.

Overhead projectiles of these activities will help students comprehend the concepts. Explain first that reading takes many forms: that although paintings or illustrations, for example, use a different "language," they can still be "read" or interpreted. In the same way, graphs and charts contain a wealth of information that needs to be unlocked before it can be understood. Use the overhead projectiles to identify the tables, pie graphs, bar graphs, and line graphs presented in this assignment. When reviewing the answers, the overhead projectiles will prove invaluable.

Discussion questions

With what kinds of information do charts seem to be most useful?
With what kinds of information do graphs seem to be most useful?
Which charts and graphs in these assignments were easiest to interpret? Why?
Which was hardest to interpret? Why?

Additional activity: Put the following information in a graph or chart: A student's marks for three terms were as follows: English: 86, 79, 58; Math: 43, 63, 55; Science: 79, 88, 89; Geography: 67, 85, 66; History: 76, 69, 63.

Activity:
"Presenting data"
pg. 53 (60 min.)

Purpose:
To reinforce students' understanding of tables, pie graphs, bar graphs, and line graphs through application activities.

Using the overhead projectiles from the previous activity, review how tables, pie graphs, and line graphs are drawn and labelled. Identify any problem areas in the assignment and use the discussion questions to ensure that students have enough guidance to begin each activity. Survey the class for color of eyes and put the numbers of each on the chalk board to be used in the third activity.

Discussion questions

What labelling will you use in your bar graphs?
How many lines will be in your line graph? What units will you use for your population labelling?
How will you find the percentage of change for the population table?

Additional activity: Survey your classmates for their favorite TV shows. Present the results in a form that best suits the data.

Activity:
"Recommended reading"
pg. 54 (40 min.)

Purpose:
To help students find a good book to read.

Most students have difficulty finding a good book. This activity is one way to assist them. No one can predict what someone else will enjoy or even be able to comprehend. Emphasize that these are merely suggestions. Distribute only the list of recommended titles; read aloud the annotated lists. The students check off the titles that seem most interesting. Their list contains blank spaces at the end for additional titles. Feel free to augment these selections with your own favorites. The discussion questions and additional activity will elicit more titles.

Discussion questions

What books have you read that you think other people might enjoy? Briefly explain what they're about.

Additional activity: Add to your list any of the titles your classmates or your teacher have suggested that you think are promising. Choose the two books you think you'd most like to try. Go to the library and sign them out.

Purpose and method

Good students are able to vary the way they read, i.e. tailor their reading strategy according to their purpose. For example if you are looking for a piece of information, it is not necessary to read a book from page 1 to the end, as you would read a story.

Five methods of reading are described below.

		Purpose
Detailed reading	Reading the whole text carefully and thoughtfully — though this doesn't have to be slowly.	Complete understanding
Reading for enjoyment	Reading at whatever pace suits you. The more you read the better reader you become.	Pleasure
Skimming	Finding out what a chapter or book is mainly about.	General impression
Scanning	Looking for specific detail by running your eye down the page quickly.	Fact finding
Detecting bias	Some people (advertisers, politicians) write to persuade. You need to separate fact from opinion.	Making up your own mind

Match the following reading tasks with the letter of the appropriate reading method:

   a. Detailed reading
   b. Reading for enjoyment
   c. Skimming
   d Scanning
   e. Detecting bias

1. Looking for a phone number in a directory. _____

2. Reading a mystery novel. _____

3. Checking a catalogue for the cheapest CD player. _____

4. Deciding whether or not to buy a costly paperback novel. _____

5. Reading a campaign brochure from a local politician. _____

6. Reading an assigned chapter in your history text. _____

7. Looking for a definition in a dictionary. _____

8. Reading an excerpt from an encyclopedia for a research project. _____

9. Reading a letter to the editor in a newspaper. _____

10. Deciding which of several books on a topic would be best to take out of the library. _____

Skimming

When you skim a page (or a chapter) you get an idea of what it's about. You do not read every word but instead you read:

1. The title and sub-headings.
2. The first sentence from each paragraph (first paragraph of the chapter).
3. The last sentence of the passage (last passage of the chapter).
4. If the chapter you are reading contains a summary, then read that first.

You should pay attention to any diagrams, charts or graphs.

Skim the passage first and then answer the questions that follow.

ENERGY

Everything that happens involves a transfer of energy. The sun has provided most of the energy which is *useful* to us.

Forms of energy transfer

There are many forms of energy transfer. These sketches show examples of the types:

Energy can be stored in the form of chemical, nuclear or potential energy: It is harder to store other forms.

Energy transfer

One form of energy transfer can lead to another. If you clap your hands, chemical energy stored in your muscles is converted to movement then sound. When you travel on a bike or in a car and the brakes are applied, movement is converted to heat in the brakes. What energy transfers take place when some paper is burned? Machines can control the rate of transfer of energy and how much useful work it does. A human is an example of a machine in which energy transfers take place.

1. The passage is about _____

   _____

   _____

2. There are approximately _____ forms of energy.

3. Machines are devices which _____

   _____

   _____

Scanning

When you scan a page or chapter, you are looking for a piece of information. You do not need to read every word but instead you should run your eye down the page fairly quickly. Scan this Periodic Table of elements to see if gold (Au) is amongst them.

H																	He
Li	Be											B	C	N	O	F	Ne
Na	Mg											Al	Si	P	S	Cl	Ar
K	Ca	Sc	Ti	V	Cr	Mn	Fe	Co	Ni	Cu	Zn	Ga	Ge	As	Se	Br	Kr
Rb	Sr	Y	Zr	Nb	Mo	Tc	Ru	Rh	Pd	Ag	Cd	In	Sn	Sb	Te	I	Xe
Cs	Ba	La	Hf	Ta	W	Re	Os	Ir	Pt	Au	Hg	Tl	Pb	Bi	Po	At	Rn

You are going to scan the passage "**The World under Water**" so that you can fill in the missing words in the three sentences. Read the sentences first.

1. If the world's ice melted the level of the sea would rise by _____ m.

2. The Antarctic summer would be _____ than the Arctic but its winters would be more _____.

3. During the warmer phases in the early part of this century some types of fish suddenly appeared off the _____ coast.

The World under Water

Since one tenth of the world is covered by ice the effect on mankind if all the ice melted would be dramatic. Most of this ice stretches across the 1,800,000 sq. km. (700,000 sq. miles) of Greenland and the 13,000,000 sq. km. (5,000,000 sq. miles) of Antarctica. If all this ice were to melt the level of the seas would rise by about 76 metres (250 feet) swamping all the world's harbours and many of its principalities. The Panama Canal would become a strait and the Suez Canal would vanish. The Bering Strait between Alaska and the USSR would widen, allowing more warm water to sweep into the Arctic and channelling cold water down the west coast of America. Most of England would vanish apart from the Cotswolds, Mendips, Chilterns and Downs. Only the tips of the New York skyscrapers would peep above the waves but Australia and Africa would be relatively unharmed. Rainfall would be re-distributed and Continental areas could experience drought. Such a melting could shift the poles and start another Ice Age due to more water vapour — and hence more snow.

But, apart from the submerging of vast areas of land, the effect would be a return to the conditions experienced just before the great Ice Ages. Air temperatures in both high and low latitudes would be very similar. The temperature of the Arctic would rise by 5-10°C in summer and by 2.5°-5°C in winter. The Antarctic summer would be warmer than the Arctic but its winters would be more severe. There could even be a return to sub-tropical vegetation in the lower latitudes and there would be mass migrations of birds and animals towards the north. The warming of the sea would have a pronounced effect on the pattern of sea life. For example, during the warmer phase of the early part of this century the cod, herring and haddock suddenly appeared off the Greenland coast. As the climate became cooler in the 1960s, the catch dropped dramatically. In some land areas there would be a big increase in the agricultural growing season.

Extract from Collins *Young Scientist*, M. Ketzner.

Reading strategies practice

On the following pages there are five passages each preceded by a question. Read the questions first because they are your purpose for reading. Decide which style of reading will be most effective for answering each question. The strategies are: detailed reading, reading for enjoyment, skimming, scanning, and detecting bias.

Write in the box at the end of each passage the reading strategy you used.

The following retelling of a traditional aboriginal folk tale explains why bears have short tails. Have you ever met anyone like the bear or the fox in this story?

Once upon a time, Bear had a long, fluffy tail just like Fox. Then came a long, cold winter. Now, Bear didn't like the cold weather. That's why he liked to sleep in the winter and wake up in the spring. Sometimes, he woke up a little too early when snow still lay on the ground and ice covered the rivers and the lake.

In the summer, Bear could just reach into the flowing water with his powerful paws and toss the wriggling fish up and out onto the bank. Fresh fish was his most favorite food! When ice covered the water, however, he didn't know what to do to fill his hungry tummy.

One day, he spied some people going out on the frozen lake. They cut a hole in the ice and began catching fish with a hook on a line tied to a wooden pole.

"What a good idea," thought Bear. "I will fish the way people do."

Bear cut a hole in the ice with his steel-like claws and reached into the icy water with his paws. He swiped this way and that but couldn't seem to find a fish anywhere.

While Bear was on his belly with his paws under the water, Fox happened along.

"What do you think you're doing?" inquired Fox.

"I'm fishing the way people do," replied Bear.

"I don't think so," said Fox. "People fish with a line not with their hands."

"Well, I don't have a line," replied Bear. "What else can I do?"

"You've got your tail," said Fox. "Why not use that for a line?"

Bear was very proud of his long, lovely tail. He twitched it back and forth and realized it would indeed make a perfect line.

"But won't I need a hook?" Bear asked.

"Of course not," scoffed Fox. "The fish will catch on to the hairs on your tail. Simply lower it through the hole in the ice and the fish will be jumping over themselves to get at such a prize as your tail."

"You're very clever, Fox," admitted Bear. "Are you clever enough to tell me how I will know when the fish are ready to be pulled up?"

"When the fish start to catch on to your tail, it will begin to feel heavy. When it feels really heavy, you'll know you've got a lot of fish attached. That's when you pull your tail out."

Bear had heard enough. He eagerly lowered his tail through the hole in the ice and sat down. Fox watched him for a while with a strange smile on his face. Then he trotted happily away.

Bear sat for a very long time, getting colder and colder, but his tail also started to get heavier and heavier.

"Well," he finally said to himself, shivering in spite of his furry coat, "I'm colder than I've ever been, but it's all been worth it. My tail feels so heavy that I'm sure to have many fish attached by now. It's time to land them!"

He jumped up, giving his tail a mighty pull, and was jerked back down again. Bear instantly realized his folly.

"Oh, no!" he cried aloud. "How could I be so stupid! Fox has tricked me and my tail is frozen solid in the ice!

In anger and frustration, he leaped and tugged and pulled and jumped, this way and that, trying to free himself from the ice. Finally, he gathered all his strength and leaped frantically into the air, breaking himself free and tumbling head over heels. Sadly, however, his frozen tail had broken in two and most of it still lay embedded in the ice.

That's why, even today, bears have little stumps for tails and why no one should ever trust a fox.

Reading Strategy used =

How do cotton fibres become yarn?

Fibres of cotton have to be disentangled before they can be worked. A pair of boards were used to do this; they were covered in leather through which hooks stuck out. One board was pulled over the other and as the fibres were loosened a sliver of 'carded' cotton was produced.

The fibres can be pulled out from each other while they are in this loose form but if they are twisted they stick together and a very strong yarn is made.

Spinning is the pulling out of just enough yarn and then twisting until the fibres are locked together in this way. All spinning machines depend on two actions. The first is that if the spindle points along the line of the yarn then as it spins it twists the yarn.

The second action is that if the yarn is pulled at right angles to the spindle and then as the spindle is spun the yarn is wound onto the spindle.

Reading Strategy used =

Is this a fair analysis of our energy supplies?

A BRIGHTER FUTURE

Fossil fuels are in short supply: oil will run out soon and though there is enough coal for 200 years we could only mine 100 years of this as the rest is far too expensive to extract. Wind, wave and solar power are romantic alternatives: they are expensive and need careful examination from a safety viewpoint. It is nice to think we can turn back the clock but we owe it to our grandchildren to provide them with the safest, cheapest and most abundant form of energy our technological society has to offer — nuclear power.

Nuclear power can provide us with all the energy we need. There is no sense in being frightened of nuclear power just because it powered the atom bomb. The safety record of the nuclear industry is excellent despite the much publicized accidents. Getting energy from atoms has proved to be very safe indeed and has nothing to do with atomic bombs.

Now is the time to call a halt to the great nuclear debate and to get on with the task of building new reactors to produce the energy of the future.

Reading Strategy used =

What can you garnish vegetarian starters with?

Vegetarian food is tasty, healthy, and better for the planet as vegetables make more productive use of land than cattle. Vegetables make excellent starters because they are neither too filling nor too rich. Soups can be prepared in advance and frozen. With a light main meal a thick soup is best, while in summer a chilled soup is delicious. When preparing soups cut the vegetables quite small to extract as much flavor as possible. There are many vegetable salads and hot starters too, such as globe artichokes with butter. Garnish soups and starters with croutons, chopped herbs, or decorative vegetables.

Reading Strategy used =

Does this passage show how bird life is threatened?

The global decline of bird populations has generally been caused by the destruction of the birds' environments. Although the destruction of wetlands is difficult to control, organizations for the saving of marsh areas, such as the Coto Danana in Spain, have occasionally been effective.

The use of harmful pesticides can be curbed by law. To reduce the possibility of oil spills, laws controlling safe tanker operation should be encouraged in every way. Many countries have some legislation that protect birds from hunters. But the enforcement ranges from negligible to adequate. In general North American birds are better protected than those in South America. In a few countries wild birds are hunted for food but usually for luxurious eating rather than as a source of necessary protein. In Britain, as a rule, all birds and their eggs are protected.

Reading Strategy used =

SQ3R: A reading strategy for assignments

Survey   Skim the passage or chapter. Is it really the one you want (the best for the job)?

Question   You might have a question to answer already or after surveying you should pose questions to focus on when you read. These questions are your reading purpose.

Read   Read carefully and pay attention to graphs, diagrams and charts. It might be better to read a section with difficult ideas twice quickly instead of once slowly. If it is your own book use a highligher pen to draw your attention to important points. You could underline words you do not understand or points you are unsure about.

Review   Has the passage answered all your questions?
Are there some parts which you need to re-read?
Look up the words you didn't understand in a dictionary. Ask your teacher about any points that are not clear to you.

Recall   Highlight or underline information you may be asked in a test or exam.

Practise SQ3R on the following passage from *Bury My Heart at Wounded Knee*, by Dee Brown, (published by Pan Paperbacks).

Survey   What is it about?

Answer _____

_____

_____

Question   1. What did the Spaniards do to the Taino and Arawak people?
2. What was Columbus' opinion of the Indians?

(Answer these questions after reading the passage i.e. at the **Review** stage.)

Review   Now answer the questions.

1. _____

_____

2. _____

_____

Recall   What methods would you use if you had to learn some of this material?

_____

_____

_____

SQ3R: A reading strategy — *continued*

Bury My Heart at Wounded Knee

It began with Christopher Columbus, who gave the people the name *Indios*. Those Europeans, the white men, spoke in different dialects, and some pronounced the word *Indien*, or *Indianer*, or Indian. *Peaux-rouges*, or redskins, came later. As was the custom of the people when receiving strangers, the Tainos on the island of San Salvador generously presented Columbus and his men with gifts and treated them with honor.

"So tractable, so peaceful, are these people," Columbus wrote to the King and Queen of Spain, "that I swear to your Majesties there is not in the world a better nation. They love their neighbors as themselves, and their discourse is ever sweet and gentle, and accompanied with a smile; and though it is true that they are naked, yet their manners are decorous and praiseworthy."

All this, of course, was taken as a sign of weakness, if not heathenism, and Columbus being a righteous European was convinced the people should be "made to work, sow and do all that is necessary and to adopt our ways". Over the next four centuries (1492-1890) several million Europeans and their descendants undertook to enforce their ways upon the people of the New World.

Columbus kidnapped ten of his friendly Taino hosts and carried them off to Spain, where they could be introduced to the white man's ways. One of them died soon after arriving there, but not before he was baptised a Christian. The Spaniards were so pleased that they had made it possible for the first Indian to enter heaven that they hastened to spread the good news throughout the West Indies.

The Tainos and other Arawak people did not resist conversion to the Europeans' religion, but they did resist strongly when hordes of these bearded strangers began scouring their islands in search of gold and precious stones. The Spaniards looted and burned villages; they kidnapped hundreds of men, women, and children and shipped them to Europe to be sold as slaves: Arawak resistance brought on the use of guns and sabers, and whole tribes were destroyed, hundreds of thousands of people in less than a decade after Columbus set foot on the beach of San Salvador, October 12, 1492.

Communications between the tribes of the New World were slow, and news of the Europeans' barbarities rarely overtook the rapid spread of new conquests and settlements. Long before the English-speaking white men arrived in Virginia in 1607, however, the Powhatans had heard rumors about the civilizing techniques of the Spaniards. The Englishmen used subtler methods. To ensure peace long enough to establish a settlement at Jamestown, they put a golden crown upon the head of Wahunsonacook, dubbed him King Powhatan, and convinced him that he should put his people to work supplying the white settlers with food.

Dee Brown

This section introduced you to different reading strategies. To become an efficient and flexible reader you must practise these skills to make them your own.

For example you can practise most of these techniques when reading a newspaper.

❏ Skim the first few pages to find which story you most want to read.

❏ Read the story carefully.

❏ Scan the classified advertisements for a bike you might like to buy.

❏ Read the newspaper's opinion column (the editorial), which is usually either on the middle page, the inside back page, or on page 2 or 4.

Can you detect bias? How much of it is fact, and how much of it is opinion?

Unlocking new vocabulary

A **prefix** is a group of letters which when put at the front of a word, changes the meaning. A **suffix** is a word ending. Knowing the meaning of some prefixes and suffixes will help you to work out the general meaning of many words.

Below is a list of prefixes in alphabetical order. The meaning of each is given. Give an example of the use of each.

Prefix	Meaning	Example
Ab	away from, out of,	*abscond*
Ad	to	_____
Ante	before	_____
Auto	self, by one's self	_____
Bene	well	_____
Bi	two, twice	_____
Cata	below, down	_____
Chron	of time	_____
Co	together	_____
Com (or con)	together, with	_____
Contra	against	_____
De	below, down	_____
Dia	through, across	_____
Dis	apart, removal	_____
En (or em)	in, into, cause to be	_____
Epi	on	_____
Ex	away from, out of	_____
Hetero	unlike	_____
Homo	same	_____
Hyper	over, in excess	_____
Hypo	below, down	_____
In (or im)	not	_____
Infra	below, beneath	_____
Inter	between, among, across, through	

Prefix	Meaning	Example
Intra	inside	_____
Mis	wrong, ill	_____
Omni	all	_____
Ortho	straight, upright, true	_____
Per	through, across, by means of	_____
Poly	many	_____
Post	after	_____
Pre	before	_____
Pro	before, in front of	_____
Quad	four	
Re	again, repeated	_____
Retro	backwards, after, behind	_____
Semi	half	_____
Sub	below, under, part of	_____
Tele	far, distant	_____
Trans	across, through	_____
Tri	three	_____

Certain suffixes indicate the function of words:

—**tion**	=	a noun
—**ly**	=	an adverb
—**ful**	=	an adjective

Interpreting data

Data is presented in a variety of ways: you must learn to recognize and understand each method of presentation and be prepared to draw conclusions about the data. You must be able to bring together data from different sources and present it in your own way. Four different types of data presentation follow:

A. Tables

Data is often presented in a table to facilitate making comparisons when dealing with large amounts of information. After studying Figure 1, answer the questions that follow.

Figure 1:

Twenty-Five Key Indicators of Social Development			
Indicators	Canada	US	Sweden
INCOME AND POVERTY			
1. Income per Person (%US)	79.0%	100.0%	70.2%
2. Poverty Rate	10.3%	17.0%	6.4%
3. Child Poverty Rate	15.5%	22.4%	2.6%
JOBS			
4. Employment Rate	71.1%	74.1%	74.2%
5. Unemployment Rate	6.8%	4.0%	5.9%
6. Working Long Hours	22.0%	26.0%	17.0%
7. Low Paid Jobs	20.9%	24.5%	5.3%
8. Earnings Gap	3.7	4.6	2.2
EMPLOYMENT SECURITY			
9. UI Benefits as % Earnings	28.0%	14.0%	29.0%
10. Jobs Supports (%GDP)	0.5%	0.2%	1.8%
11. Unionization Rate	36.0%	18.0%	89.0%
SOCIAL SUPPORTS			
12. Health Care (Public Share)	69.6%	44.7%	83.8%
13. Tertiary Education (Public Share)	60.0%	51.0%	91.0%
14. Private Social Spending	4.5%	8.6%	3.0%
HEALTH			
15. Life Expectancy (Men)	75.3	72.5	75.9
16. Life Expectancy (Women)	81.3	79.2	81.3
17. Infant Mortality/100,000	5.5	7.2	3.5
CRIME			
18. Homicides per 100,000	1.8	5.5	NA
19. Assault/Threat per 100,000	4.0	5.7	4.2
20. Prisoners per 100,000	118	546	71
EDUCATION			
21. Adults/Post Secondary Ed.	38.8%	34.9%	28.0%
22. High Literacy (% Adults)	25.1%	19.0%	35.5%
23. Low Literacy (% Adults)	42.9%	49.6%	25.1%
24. Grade 12 Math Score	519	461	552
CIVIC PARTICIPATION			
25. Voter Turnout	56.2%	49.1%	83.2%

Source: Canadian Council on Social Development

Twenty-five Key Indicators of Social Development

Answer the following questions.

1. a. If you wanted to make the most money, in which country should you work?
    b. In which country would you find the lowest levels of poverty of all kinds? What are incomes like in this country?
2. a. Which country has the lowest paying jobs and workers who work the longest hours?
    b. Which country has the highest unemployment rate?
3. Which country has the highest number of unionized workers? Which has the lowest?
4. What does the table tell you about how health care and education are paid for in Sweden?
5. In what country would you have the greatest chance of living the longest? The least chance of living the longest?
6. What does the table tell you in general about crime in the U.S. compared to the other two countries?
7. What does the table tell you in general about literacy in the three countries?
8. In which country would you expect the greatest voter turnout?

B. Pie Graphs

The proportions in a pie graph allow comparisons to be made in the flick of an eye. The whole pie equals 100%.

Figure 2: Marital Status of Persons 15 Years and Over, by Sex: 1990, United States.

Answer the following questions.

1. Which gender has the greatest chance of getting married? How much greater?

2. How do you account for the differences in the divorce and separation rates between the genders?

3. What can you tell about the number of men compared to the number of women? How did you come to your conclusion?

4. What can you tell about the life expectancy of men and women? How did you come to your conclusion?

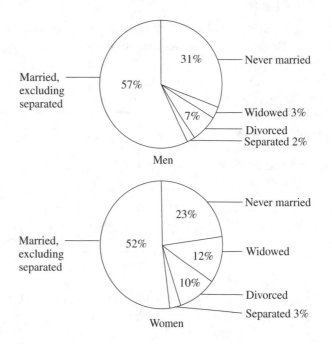

C. Bar graphs

Bar graphs allow instant comparisons among a relatively large number of items.

Figure 3:

Figure 4:

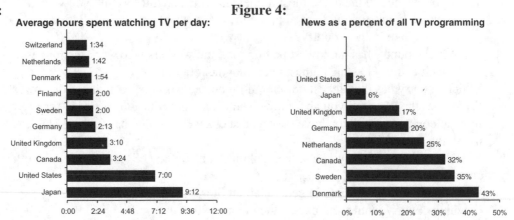

1. In which country do people watch the most TV per day? In which country do people watch the least TV per day?
2. Which country has the largest percentage of news programming? Which country has the least?
3. Look at figures 3 and 4 for Japan and the United States. What conclusions can you draw about the viewing habits in these two countries?

D. Line graphs

Line graphs are usually used to make comparisons over time with a small number of items. Examine Figure 5 and answer the questions below.

Figure 5:
Sources of revenue for U.S. public elementary and secondary schools: 1970–71 to 1998–99

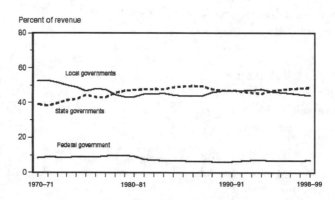

1. In the early 70s, which level of government provided the most money for education? Which level of government provided the least?
2. In the late 90s, which level of government provided the most money for education? Which level of government provided the least?
3. From the information in the graph, what can you say about the participation of the federal government (two points)?
4. What can you tell about local and state participation in 1978 and 1989?

Presenting data

Figure 6: Average price of a gallon of gas:

Sweden	$4.85
Denmark	4.46
United Kingdom	3.56
Germany	3.05
Netherlands	3.02
Japan	3.01
Canada	1.40
United States	1.07

1. Create a bar graph to demonstrate the average price of a gallon of gas in the countries indicated.

Figure 7: Population projections for Canada 10–14 year-olds

Population in millions

Year	Male	Female
2000	1.1	1.0
2025	1.05	1.0
2050	1.05	1.05

15–19 year-olds

2000	1.1	1.025
2025	1.5	1.05
2050	1.1	1.08

2. Create a line graph to demonstrate the population projections from 2000 to 2050.
3. Survey your classmates for color of eyes. Turn your data into a pie graph.

Figure 8: Population for selected states

State	Population 1990	Population 2000	Numeric Change 1990–2000	Percent 1990–2000
United States	248 709 873	281 421 906		
Alaska	550 043	626 932		
Colorado	3 294 394	4 301 261		
Florida	12 937 926	15 982 378		
Hawaii	1 108 229	1 211 537		
Iowa	2 776 755	2 926 324		
Maine	1 227 928	1 274 923		
North Carolina	6 628 637	8 049 313		
Oregon	2 842 321	3 421 399		
Texas	16 986 510	20 851 820		
Washington	4 866 692	5 894 121		

4. For the population data given above, complete the table by filling in the numeric change from 1990 to 2000, and the percentage change from 1990 to 2000.

Recommended reading

The following selection of celebrated books points you in the direction of material that other people have found enriching and enlightening. While these books are recommended, they are only suggestions. Our individual backgrounds, experiences, interests, and purposes for reading vary so significantly that you will have to make up your own mind about how appropriate a selection might be for you. Your teacher will supply you with a brief synopsis of each selection to give you an idea of the books you might like to try initially.

Please place a check mark beside the selections that look promising:

Fiction for Mature Students

❑ William Bell: *Stones*
❑ Rick Book: *Necking With Louise*
❑ Ben Bova: *The Duelling Machine*
❑ Martha Brooks: *True Confessions of a Heartless Girl*
❑ Peter Carter: *Bury the Dead*
❑ Robert Cormier: *The Chocolate War*
❑ Robert Cormier: *Beyond the Chocolate War*
❑ Peter Dickinson: *Eva*
❑ Minfong Ho: *Rice Without Rain*
❑ Janni Howker: *Badger on the Barge*
❑ Tim Wynne-Jones: *The Maestro*
❑ John Knowles: *A Separate Peace*
❑ Louise Lawrence: *Children of the Dust*
❑ Bernard MacLaverty: *Cal*
❑ Kevin Major: *Hold Fast*
❑ Jan Mark: *The Ennead*
❑ Michelle Magorian: *Goodnight Mr. Tom*
❑ Jan Needle: *Piggy in the Middle*
❑ George Orwell: *Animal Farm*
❑ Morton Rhue: *The Wave*
❑ J.D. Salinger: *The Catcher in the Rye*
❑ Alexander Solzhenitsyn: *One Day in the Life of Ivan Denisovitch*
❑ Susan Terris: *Nell's Quilt*
❑ Cynthia Voigt: *Homecoming*
❑ James Watson: *Talking in Whispers*
❑ Robert Westall: *The Scarecrows*

Recommended reading — *continued*

Fiction for Younger Students

- ❑ Brian Doyle: *Uncle Ronald*
- ❑ Julie Johnston: *Hero of Lesser Causes*
- ❑ Deborah Hautzig: *Second Star to the Right*
- ❑ Robert Leeson: *It's My Life*
- ❑ Kit Pearson: *Awake and Dreaming*
- ❑ Virginia Frances Schwartz: *If I Just Had Two Wings*
- ❑ Arthur Slade: *Dust*
- ❑ Robert Swindells: *Brother in the Land*
- ❑ Jean Ure: *A Proper Little Nooryeff*
- ❑ Paul Zindell: *The Undertaker's Gone Bananas*

Non Fiction

- ❑ Valerie Avery: *London Morning*
- ❑ Gerald Durrell: *My Family And Other Animals*
- ❑ Priscilla Galloway: *Too Young to Fight*
- ❑ John Hershey: *Hiroshima*
- ❑ Paul Mattheissen: *The Snow Leopard*
- ❑ Ved Mehta: *Vedi*
- ❑ Simon Tookoome, Sheldon Oberman: *The Shaman's Nephew*
- ❑ _____
- ❑ _____
- ❑ _____
- ❑ _____
- ❑ _____
- ❑ _____
- ❑ _____
- ❑ _____
- ❑ _____
- ❑ _____

Reading list summaries

Fiction for Mature Students

William Bell: *Stones.* Garnet Havelock is in his last year at high school and is just biding his time until he is finished with the place. Always a loner, Garnet has never cared that he didn't fit in with the rest of the crowd. Then a new girl comes to the school and everything changes. As he tries to win her over, another girl vies for his attention. The trouble is, she has been dead for more than 150 years. When Garnet delves into her past he uncovers a horrible secret about the town he lives in. Layered with complex themes, *Stones* is a stimulating and at times, disturbing read.

Rick Book: *Necking With Louise.* Through a series of linked short stories a portrait of Eric emerges. At a time when he is struggling to make meaning of his life Eric discovers, through a series of deeply moving events, that he has choices to make if he is going to steer his own life. But living in the prairie West doesn't make those choices easy. Stories include: *The Clodhopper's Halloween Ball*, *The Game*, *Sundogs*, *The River*, *Saying Goodbye to the Tall Man*.

Ben Bova: *The Duelling Machine.* Conflict is abolished in this futuristic world by a machine which makes fantasy reality. Two people can share a dream world in which they can fight with any weapon.

Martha Brooks: *True Confessions of a Heartless Girl.* When 17-year-old Norene Stall comes to town she's on the run. Seems she's stolen her boyfriend's truck and a fistful of money along with his heart — oh, yes, and she's pregnant. But in an effort to leave her mistakes behind, fiercely independent Norene has a profound effect on the people in Pembina Lake, Manitoba who take her under their wings and into their hearts. A poignant and insightful tale of ordinary, yet remarkable people.

Peter Carter: *Bury The Dead.* Set in East Berlin before The Wall came down. The novel centres around the Norden family, especially Erika, who is a promising high jumper with a glittering future ahead of her. Then from the horrors of Germany's past comes Uncle Karl, long believed to be dead. Painful and awful secrets are disturbed and the future can never be the same again.

Robert Cormier: *The Chocolate War.* A high school has a secret society which bullies and manipulates its victims. The gang's newest victim, however, is no pushover.

Robert Cormier: *Beyond the Chocolate War.* A sequel to the above. Brother Leon is now headmaster of Trinity High and Archie, leader of the Vigils Secret Society, is more powerful than ever. For Obie, once Archie's right-hand and now his enemy, the destruction of Archie is vital and slowly the pattern for revenge takes shape.

Peter Dickinson: *Eva.* A strong story set in the near future. Eva awakens in hospital after a terrible accident to find herself transformed. The story startlingly dramatizes the threat to the environment from our activities.

Minfong Ho: *Rice Without Rain.* Set in Thailand, this novel looks at the way poverty is used to subdue a population. Jinda lives in a village which gives up fifty per cent of its rice crop to landowners — until students from Bangkok University incite villagers to rebel. The student intervention brings romance for Jinda but bloody consequences for her village.

Janni Howker: *Badger on the Barge.* An absorbing gallery of characters is created in these five stories, each of which is concerned with a significant encounter between two people — one young, one old.

Tim Wynne-Jones: *The Maestro.* At age 14 Burl Crow has headed into Ontario's north woods in an effort to escape his father's brutality, when he sees a strange sight overhead — a grand piano being flown by helicopter. Eventually he discovers the isolated cabin of a musical genius, Nathaniel Gow. Eccentric though he is, Nathaniel intrigues and inspires Burl as they share the refuge of the cabin. But when Nathaniel leaves Burl alone to go to Toronto for a few days, dreams of a secure future end. Gow has died in the city and Burl must use his encounter with the maestro to truly leave his past behind.

John Knowles: *A Separate Peace.* A powerful novel. It is the story of a friendship between two 16-year old boys in an American boarding school. One is an athlete and the other a scholar. Their different attitudes and outlook cause considerable tensions.

Louise Lawrence: *Children of the Dust.* The alarm bells ringing at Sarah Harnden's school signify the start of a nuclear war. The first section of this novel deals with Sarah's struggle to ensure the survival of the one member of her family most fitted for it — her stepsister Catherine. A gripping story which warns us with a frightening view of a possible future.

Bernard MacLaverty: *Cal.* A moving story of love and hate set against the troubles of Ulster. Cal, a young Catholic, falls in love with a young Protestant widow whose husband he has recently helped to murder.

Kevin Major: *Hold Fast.* Michael turned 14 in May. By June, both his parents were dead. From the moment the car crash claimed their lives, Michael is set on a new path. He will be uprooted from his small Newfoundland outport community, and sent to live in a city hundreds of miles away with relatives he hardly even knows. His struggle to survive in his new environment and his fight to retain his pride and way of life, make a gripping, unforgettable tale of sorrow, tenacity, and joy.

Jan Mark: *The Ennead.* A superb science fiction story set on a corrupt and barren planet. Isaac, a steward, thinks that his schemes are working well for him until he makes the decision to rescue a woman from a dying planet — someone who will owe him everything. But when she arrives Eleanor is far from grateful.

Michelle Magorian: *Goodnight Mister Tom.* Young Willie Beech is evacuated to the country as Britain prepares for the Second World War. He is a sad, deprived child, who begins to flourish under the care of old Tom Oakley. His new found happiness is shattered when his mother summons him back to London. A gripping story.

Jan Needle: *Piggy in the Middle.* Sandra is in the police force and her boyfriend, Dave, is a journalist. They find themselves working on the same murder case but from different angles. This causes conflicting loyalties and tensions in the relationship.

George Orwell: *Animal Farm.* The animals at Mr. Jones' farm revolt. However when the pigs take charge, one tyranny has simply replaced another. This short book is a satire on the Russian Revolution.

Morton Rhue: *The Wave.* Ben Ross is a history teacher who involves his class in an experiment. Through showing his students how the Nazis, a minority group, were allowed to dominate Germany, he exposes the powerful forces of group pressure. A gripping book in which characters are destroyed and changed in a way that is uncontrollable.

J D Salinger: *The Catcher in the Rye.* The uncompromising story of Holden Caulfield, an adolescent tired of the phoniness of modern America. He drifts in New York. The book is still banned in schools in many parts of America.

Alexander Solzhenitsyn: *One Day in the Life of Ivan Denisovitch.* Based on the author's own imprisonment, this relates the daily struggles of a prisoner in one of Stalin's camps.

Susan Terris: *Nell's Quilt.* Set in America in 1899. Nell finally agrees to marry the widower her parents have chosen for her. She has to give up her dream of going to college and following in her suffragist grandmother's footsteps. Nell begins to embroider a quilt, she stops eating and as the quilt gets bigger Nell gets frailer, losing touch with reality. A moving and disturbing tale.

Cynthia Voigt: *Homecoming.* Four children, inexplicably abandoned by their mother in a car park, need a home. Dicey, the eldest, leads them across America to find a grandmother they have never met. Its sequel, *Dicey's Song*, looks at the scars left by the incident and the adjustments the children make as they learn to trust again.

James Watson: *Talking in Whispers.* This gripping political thriller is set in Chile under the military junta. Sixteen-year-old Andres and his friends are wanted by the dreaded security forces. More than a story of oppression, this is a celebration of the bravery of those who resist.

Robert Westall: *The Scarecrows.* Simon's new stepfather causes him to run away from home. He escapes to an old water mill where Simon finds troubles of the past brought to the present. Three scarecrows appear to be following him across the field each day with an evil force. Will he have the power to stop them?

Fiction for Younger Students

Brian Doyle: *Uncle Ronald.* Though Mickey is 112 and cannot remember much, he can remember exactly what happened a century ago when he and his mother ran away from his abusive father. Luckily for Mickey he found warmth and safety with his two aunts and his Uncle Ronald in their home in the Gatineau Hills. And when Mickey's violent father finally tracked them down, Uncle Ronald and his horse, Second Chance Lance, found a way for Mickey to live another hundred years. With larger than life characters and his typical sense of humor, Brian Doyle tells an unforgettable story of hope and humanity.

Julie Johnston: *Hero of Lesser Causes.* Keely is 12 years old and knows that she has a special mission in life; to fight for Great Causes. But she is in no hurry to prove herself until tragedy strikes her family. When her brother contracts polio, Keely realizes that she may never have a greater cause than to inspire him to live. But her spirit and faith in herself will be tested as she encourages Patrick to fight for his life.

Deborah Hautzig: *Second Star to the Right.* Leslie Hiller believes her life would be so much better if only she was thinner. This a compelling read about the effects of anorexia nervosa.

Robert Leeson: *It's My Life.* When Jan's mother disappears without explanation, Jan is expected to take her place in the family while also coping with her examinations and a boyfriend.

Kit Pearson: *Awake and Dreaming.* Theo lives with her young mother in poverty and despair. She dreams of having a real family with two parents, siblings, and someone who will take responsibility for her. When the dream comes true she is happy for a time. Adopted by the Kaldors into a large, loving family, Theo has everything she has ever longed for. Then the dream comes to an end. Back with her mother, Theo's waking hours are haunted by a shadowy figure. Worse, she can no longer determine if the Kaldors were real or imagined. This is a ghost story with a difference.

Virginia Frances Schwartz: *If I Just Had Two Wings.* Thirteen-year-old Phoebe has always dreamed of a better life than the one she has as a plantation slave, but never dares to think of escape — until she meets Liney. Liney is full of stories about the Underground Railroad and the clues found in songs that will guide them all the way to Canada. When Phoebe and Liney decide they can wait no longer, they run with Liney's two small children. Along the way, they meet Jake, another runaway. Plagued by separation, illness, and harsh cold, the group is inspired by Phoebe's unflagging dreams of freedom.

Arthur Slade: *Dust.* When Robert's mother asks him to go with his little brother to buy gum, Robert refuses. So Matthew goes all by himself — and is never seen again. In the awful days that follow, Robert, wracked with guilt, tries to find Matthew and figure out why all the strange things are happening on his farm — especially why his parents are lost in a dream where they have no memory of Matthew. It becomes his mission to keep Matthew alive in their memories, and that mission leads ever closer to the dangerous stranger, Abram Harish.

Robert Swindells: *Brother in the Land.* When Danny survives a nuclear attack he has to learn to live in a world which is unimaginably and hideously altered. Others, too, are battling for survival against fallout, illness, the Authorities and each other.

Jean Ure: *A Proper Little Nooryeff.* Jamie is incapable of saying "no" which is why he finds himself in his young sister's dance class. Quite an achievement for someone who thinks dancers are sissies and who has to withstand the jeers and taunts of his school friends.

Paul Zindel: *The Undertaker's Gone Bananas.* A comic thriller in which two teenagers witness an undertaker murdering his wife.

Non-Fiction

Valerie Avery: *London Morning*. This autobiography, written when she was 16, is a lively and funny account of growing up in London in the 1940s and 1950s. Valerie's father was killed in the war, and Valerie's mother struggles to bring Valerie up in a house shared with grandparents. One of the best moments is when she brings her first boyfriend home.

Gerald Durrell: *My Family and Other Animals*. At the age of ten Gerald Durrell went with his family to Corfu. This is his story of their five years on the island. We read about the wildlife he discovered, the people he met and his relationships with his somewhat eccentric family and with a succession of tutors. It is not a traditional autobiography: the incidents related are all carefully chosen to introduce us to the fascinating animals Gerry brought into the Durrell household, and to the chaos and confusion they created for his long-suffering family.

Priscilla Galloway (Ed.): *Too Young To Fight: Memories of Our Youth During World War II*. Eleven of Canada's best authors of teen literature gather to recount their feelings and impressions about coming of age in one of the world's most tumultuous eras. Richly illustrated with personal photographs and archival material, the collection is at once funny, tragic, and insightful. Different backgrounds and locations bring a broad awareness to our own participation in, and treatment of, a world at war. Contributors include: Roch Carrier, Monica Hughes, Joy Kogawa, Brian Doyle, Janet Lunn, Claire Mackay, Jean Little.

John Hersey: *Hiroshima*. A powerful and moving account by Time Magazine's wartime correspondent.

Paul Mattheissen: *The Snow Leopard*. An account of a man's journey to find the snow leopards in the Himalayan Mountains of Pakistan and Nepal; a poetic pilgrimage full of vivid descriptions.

Ved Mehta: *Vedi*. The true story of a blind Indian writer's childhood. Ved came from a privileged background yet in the 1930s he is placed in the Bombay School for the Blind — a deprived school in the heart of one of the poorest cities. A wonderful book.

Simon Tookoome, Sheldon Oberman: *The Shaman's Nephew: A Life in the Far North*. When Sheldon Oberman met Inuit artist/hunter Simon Tookoome, a remarkable collaboration began. Over the next decade and through countless tapes and translations the two would record the customs and beliefs of a rapidly disappearing way of life. Tookoome is one of the last of his people to live in the traditional, nomadic style. His voice transports readers to a cold, harsh land that warms and grows more familiar with every word. Illustrated with his own artwork, this wise, humorous, and poignant treasury touches upon many things including birth, migration, shamanism, survival, and death.

Unit 5

Learning

Many students mistakenly believe that learning occurs through a kind of osmosis; and that it either happens or it doesn't. Too often they tend to limit what they think they can achieve, or live down to their own expectations. When they're taught to evaluate where they are, set goals for where they want to be, and apply proven strategies to help them get there, the process can be a revelation. When they can then apply those strategies across the curriculum, those strategies become second nature.

Activity:
"Understanding memory"
pg. 63   (15 min.)

"Memory tricks"
pg. 64   (40 min.)

Purpose:
To help students understand and improve their use of memorization.

A significant amount of rote learning is involved in what students are asked to do in schools. Students need to discriminate between understanding concepts and rote memorization and accordingly adjust their approach to the learning. The first student activity instructs students to reflect on the kinds of memory tasks their different school subjects require. The second activity practises some simple but useful mnemonics. The discussion questions can be used to introduce the unit.

Discussion questions

What is the hardest kind of material to memorize? Why?
When you have to memorize a list of facts, how do you go about it?
When you have to understand a concept, what do you do?

Additional activity: When you next make a note that contains information you think will be required on a future test, review the mnemonics in these exercises and apply the ones most useful for the task.

Activity:
"Roadblocks to learning"
pg. 65   (20 min.)

Purpose:
To identify common roadblocks to learning.

This activity asks students to reflect on whether or not their approach to learning is affected by three common roadblocks. This activity can be paired with the activity, "Concentration and motivation," when students need to find ways around these obstacles to learning. The discussion questions can be used to review some of the roadblock concepts.

Discussion questions

What surprised you about the information on memory? How might that affect your approach to your school work?
What surprised you about the information on reviewing your work? What implications does the information have to the way you conduct your reviews?

Additional activity: After examining the common roadblocks to learning, write down the specific changes you intend to make in the way you approach your work and study habits.

Activity:
"Concentration and motivation"
pg. 66 (20 min.)

Purpose:
To help students improve their concentration and motivation.

Everyone at one time or another has difficulty with concentration and motivation. Most students don't realize that they can take practical steps to improve both. Use the discussion questions to introduce the activity.

Discussion questions

What do you do if you really aren't interested in some part of your school work?
What do you do if you can't concentrate when you know you have to?
How much should you worry about how well you're doing?

Additional activity: Make a list of the suggestions you intend to implement in your efforts to improve your concentration and motivation.

Activity:
"Pinpointing your problems"
pg. 67 (40 min.)

Purpose:
To help students analyze their strengths and weaknesses with regard to learning and develop strategies for improvement.

Introduce the idea of a bubble chart on the chalk board by placing the word "memorizing" in a circle. Ask the students to recall some of the essential points from their work with mnemonics; as they offer suggestions, link them up in bubbles to the central bubble. The first half of the student activity helps students discover their strengths and weakness with learning and the second half asks them to reflect on possible solutions for their problems. The discussion questions help them sum up their conclusions.

Discussion questions

What problems seemed to crop up in more than one subject area?
What kinds of problems are the hardest to solve?
If you have difficulty solving a particular problem yourself, who could you approach for assistance?

Additional activity: Choose one of your solutions and incorporate it into a plan for improvement. Write down the subject area, what you intend to do, and the amount of time you need to test your solution, for example, two weeks. Tell how you intend to evaluate whether or not your solution worked.

Activity:
"Achievers and underachievers"
pg. 68 (40 min.)

Purpose:
To encourage students to self-reflect on the qualities they need to continue to improve.

Introduce the activity with the discussion questions. The questions revolve around section A of the student activity sheet. The additional activity asks students to extend the exercise by reflecting on their own personal situation.

Discussion questions

How would you explain in your own words what each quality means?
What application, if any, would each one have in a school situation?

Additional activity: Choose two qualities you would like to improve in yourself. List the ways in which you could apply those qualities in your daily school life. Be as specific as you can.

Activity:
"Reflections on learning"
pg. 69 (40 min.)

Purpose:
To afford students an opportunity to internalize the importance of learning.

Learning doesn't stop when school ends. Learning and living are two sides to the same coin. Since the beginning of recorded history people have reflected on the essential nature of life-long learning. In this activity, students compare what others have said about learning with the experiences from their own lives. To introduce the topic, read aloud the letter at the top of the student activity sheet and direct students to the first question. The discussion questions can be used at the conclusion of the activity.

Discussion questions

With which saying did you most strongly agree? Why?
With which saying did you most strongly disagree? Why?

Additional activity: Write a journal entry explaining what learning means to you and how you hope to continue to learn throughout your life.

Understanding memory

We have two types of memory:

  short term memory
  long term memory.

When we first learn something it enters our short term memory, a sort of hotel reception where it stays until a room is found for it. If the piece of information *links up* to something already in the brain it is quickly brought in and given a resting place. If the information proves useful, like a friend's telephone number, and is *used*, then it is transferred to our long term memory. If information is not linked up, or used again, then it will slip out of the short term memory.

It is much easier to remember things which you understand.

Most school subjects require you to memorize information. In which school subjects does your memory work best?

_____

Which school subjects are hardest to learn?

_____

Can you explain the difference in your performance in these subjects? There may be many reasons. List the most important ones.

(a) _____

_____

(b) _____

_____

(c) _____

_____

(d) _____

_____

(e) _____

_____

Memory tricks

Mnemonics (ne mon´ ics) are devices and techniques to improve memory. Simple mnemonics are useful when trying to memorize facts. In the following examples, a simple phrase is memorized and the initial letter of each word is the same letter that begins a word you need to remember.

A. Please complete both examples below.

Great Lakes	**Planets**
Some _____	Many _____
Men _____	Very _____
Hate _____	Eager _____
Each _____	Mermaids _____
Other _____	Jumped _____
	Splash _____
	Under _____
	Nearby _____
	Pools _____

B. From your own notes, choose five groups of difficult-to-remember facts. Create your own mnenomic phrases to help you remember them. Write them on the back of this sheet.

C. Explain how you might use the following techniques to help you remember.

● Color coding _____

_____

● Highlighting _____

_____

● Check marks _____

_____

● Numbering _____

_____

● Reciting _____

_____

● Writing _____

_____

Roadblocks to learning

A. Information may not be taken in very well.

Are your study habits good? _____

Are you well organized and studying in good conditions? _____

Do you study when you are fresh and alert? _____

Do you make clear notes which you understand before learning? _____

Do you break large pieces of work into smaller units? _____

Do you reorganize your work, underlining key words and ideas? _____

B. New information is not used.

This graph shows how much people can remember after different lengths of time.
Answer these questions:

About how much information is

(a) never recalled? _____%
(b) recorded in the short term memory?
    _____%
(c) recorded in the long term memory?
    _____%

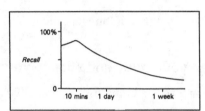

To *remember* what you have learned try to apply your new knowledge to different situations.
Questions make you think about what you have learned.

Once you have understood the work you can decide which parts you need to commit to your long term memory. The shape of the graph changes if you review your work.

Answer these questions:

About how much information is

(a) learned at each review? _____%

(b) stored in the long term memory after a
    week? _____%

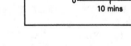

Use your daily planner to remind you to
review work regularly:
    ❏ the day after making the notes   ❏ every half term

C. New information is not linked to existing knowledge.

You may have noticed the first part of the curve in each of the graphs above shows an increase in recall 10 minutes after studying has stopped. This is probably because your brain needs some time to absorb what has been learned, and to link it to what you already know. After this has been done the work makes more sense and is easier to recall. If you don't understand work then this bonus is lost and the slope of the forgetting curve will be even steeper for you.

Inaccurate notes mislead you and make complete understanding of a topic very difficult. Without understanding, notes become almost impossible to learn.

Concentration and motivation

1. Take an interest in your subject

This can help to bring it alive for you. Try to make connections between what you are studying and your everyday life. For example you know an atom is made up of protons, neutrons and electrons, but next time you are watching the television consider that it is the electrons hitting the other side of the screen which produce the image you see.

2. Set yourself realistic goals

and work rapidly towards them. Examples of short term goals are:

❏ planning an essay

❏ working from 7:30 to 8 p.m.

❏ completing one stage of a project.

Gaining a diploma is a long term goal. Write down your long term goals.

3. Plan your study and stick to your plans

A regular place and time for study help you to settle down quickly to your work.

4. Vary your approach to study

If you approach a topic or problem from more than one angle you are more likely to understand it. Your brain likes variety. Active methods of learning help you to concentrate.

5. Distractions destroy concentration

Keep your books, files, and equipment in one place so that you don't waste time looking for things. Tell your family when you are studying so that you won't be disturbed.

6. Worrying about something can spoil your concentration

If you can't understand something make a note of it and ask about it. Then you can get on with the rest of your work, but always understand work before having to memorize it.

7. Check your progress

Record teachers' comments (and grades). If you see that you are achieving your goals then you will be more motivated to continue your study.

8. Put your knowledge to work as often as you can.

Pinpointing your problems

A. Decide which of your school subjects you find the easiest and which you find the most difficult. Create a bubble chart for each to help explain why you find more success in one than the other. The subject is the center bubble. Use as many bubbles as you need. An example has been started below:

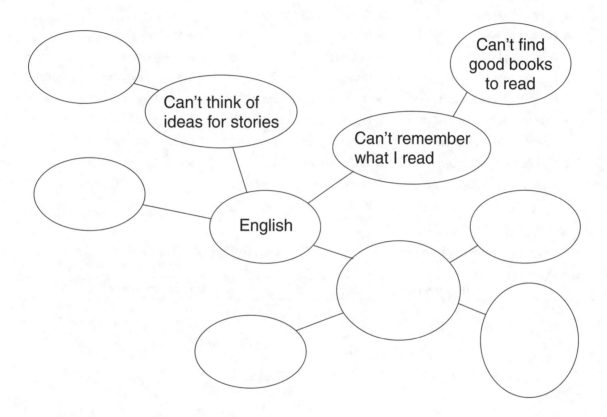

B. Create other bubble charts based on the one you made for the subject you find most difficult. Choose one of the problems you identified and put it in the center. Surround the center bubble with steps you can take to solve the problem. Create as many bubble charts as you have problems.

Achievers and underachievers

Whether or not they do well at school, some people make a good start at work and continue to improve. Others don't seem to be able to improve. Below is a list of 26 qualities: some shown by improvers, some shown by non-improvers.

A. Discuss what you think each one means.

- Poor timekeeping
- Doesn't try hard
- Asks questions
- Can't concentrate
- Careless about presentation
- Takes pride in work
- Doesn't follow instructions
- Co-operates with others
- Works when unsupervised

- Dislikes people in charge
- Reports faults
- Punctual
- Solves problems
- Does not like change
- Doesn't report problems
- Personal problems
- Wide viewpoint
- Doesn't get on with other people

- Versatile
- Methodical and neat
- Wastes time
- No loyalty to the organization
- Listens to instructions
- Takes initiative
- Over-confident
- Quality-conscious

B. Sort out the qualities into these two columns. (There are 13 qualities for each.)

Achievers	Underachievers

C. Suggest how the qualities for achievers could be applied in school.

_____

_____

_____

_____

_____

_____

Reflections on learning

Chicago, October 1, 189-

Dear Pierrepont

Your Ma got back safe this morning and she wants me to be sure to tell you not to over-study, and I want to tell you not to under-study. What we're really sending you to Harvard for is to get a little of the education that's so good and plenty there. When it's passed around you don't want to be bashful, but reach right out and take a big helping every time, for I want you to get your share. You'll find that education's about the only thing lying around loose in this world, and that it's about the only thing a fellow can have as much of as he's willing to haul away. Everything else is screwed down tight and the screwdriver lost.

Of course, a man should have a certain amount of play, just as a boy is entitled to a piece of pie at the end of his dinner, but he don't want to make a meal of it.

George Horace Lorimer, Letters from a self-made merchant to his son (1902)

"Only the educated are free." *Epictetus*, 2nd century
"Who neglects learning in youth, loses the past and is dead for the future." *Euripides*, 412 BC
"Much learning does not teach understanding." *Heraclitus*, c 500 BC
"Education is not a product: mark, diploma, job, money — in that order; it is a process, a never-ending one."
   Bel Kaufman, 1967
"The direction in which education starts a man, will determine his future life." *Plato*, 4th century BC
"An inch of gold cannot buy an inch of time." *Chinese proverb*
"It is only the ignorant who despise education." *Publilius Syrus*, 1st century BC
"Few things are impossible to diligence and skill." *Samuel Johnson*, 1759
"When we do the best that we can, we never know what miracle is wrought in our lives, or in the life of
   another." *Helen Keller*, 1913
"No one knows what he can do till he tries." *Publilius Syrus*, 1st century BC
"I like work; it fascinates me. I can sit and look at it for hours. I love to keep it by me: the idea of getting rid
   of it nearly breaks my heart." *Jerome K Jerome, Three Men in a Boat* (1889)
"When a man's education is finished, he is finished." *E A Filene*, (1860-1937)
"I hear and I forget
   I see and I remember
   I do and I understand." *Chinese Proverb*
"The palest ink is better than the sharpest memory." *Chinese Proverb*
"It's not enough to be busy. The question is: What are you busy about?" *Henry Thoreau* (1817-62)

Reflections on learning: Activities

1. Read the letter that begins "Dear Pierrepont." Explain in your own words what the advice means. Identify whether you tend to "under-study" or "over-study" and explain how your behavior supports how you view yourself.
2. Choose the saying that best describes someone you know. Explain why that person fits the saying.
3. Choose a saying that describes an encounter you've had with learning. Describe that encounter and tell why the saying is so appropriate.
4. Choose the saying with which you disagree the most. Explain why you disagree.
5. Choose a saying and change it so that it means the exact opposite. How much truth is in the opposite meaning?
6. Choose a saying that best fits one of your teachers. Who is the teacher and why is the saying so apt?

Unit 6

Writing Essays

After the freedom of narrative and poetic writing, students usually find the constrictions of the essay form challenging. When the purpose for the writing changes from personal expression to persuasion or instruction, the thinking that supports effective writing must become more carefully structured. Successful argumentation requires linkages in content from statement of thesis through substantiating propositions, a chain of reasoning, and a logical consistency producing a unified whole. Needless to say, students appreciate step-by-step direction as they attempt to master the form.

Activity:
  "Planning an essay"
  pg. 73   (40 min.)

Purpose:
  To instruct students in how to plan an argumentative essay.

Effective essay writing stems from having something to say. Writing an essay must begin with reflecting on what it is you want to say and then deciding how best to say it. This activity provides students with a practical way to gather ideas about a subject and explore how those ideas are linked. The discussion questions can be used in conjunction with the five styles of writing listed at the beginning of the student activity to introduce the theme.

Discussion questions

When in school have you used each of the different styles of writing?
Which style have you used most often? Why?
Which style requires the least planning? Why?

Additional activity: List five topics about which you have a lot of opinions or knowledge. Create a title for each one that would engage or intrigue someone else.

Activity:
  "Beginning an essay"
  pg. 74   (40 min.)

Purpose:
  To help students explore writing effective opening sentences.

Opening sentences are crucial to "hooking" the reader; not surprisingly, they're the most difficult to compose. This activity asks students to discriminate among a number of opening sentences before they attempt to write their own. The discussion questions can be used to introduce the topic.

Discussion questions

What movie or television program opened in such a way that you were "hooked" from the beginning? How did it start?
What different emotions can be appealed to when opening an essay?

Additional activity: Go back to the topics and titles you created after the planning activity. Choose the one you like most and write five opening sentences for that title. Which opening do you think is most effective? Why?

Activity:
"Revising an essay"
pg. 77   (40 min.)

Purpose:
To help students develop revising skills.

Use the discussion questions to lead into the topic of revising. Students will often use editing and revising interchangeably. They need to understand the difference between the two activities. They also need to understand that of the two skills revising is the most important and the most difficult. When students are word processing, spell check and grammar check are almost automatic activities. They also need to appreciate that although editing often begins with the computer checking features, much more is required.

Discussion questions

What's the difference between revising and rewriting?
What's the difference between editing and revising? Which one is more difficult? Why?

Additional activity: Go back to a piece of writing you wrote near the beginning of the term or even the school year. Read it over. If you had the chance to write it over again, what changes would you make? Why?

Activity:
"Evaluating an essay"
pg. 78   (40 min.)

Purpose:
To help students learn how to evaluate an essay.

If students would just put their completed writing away for at least a few days before handing it in, they'd be able to look at it with fresh and more objective eyes. If they could get someone else to offer an objective and truthful critique, they would also be able to make some necessary revisions before submitting it for evaluation. Begin the session by eliciting from the students why both these approaches are so difficult to put into practice. The discussion questions would serve to sum up the unit activities after the students have completed them.

Discussion questions

What comments would you put on Alison's essay if you were the teacher?
What mark would you give Alison? How would you justify that mark?

Additional activity: Go back to several pieces of writing you wrote near the beginning of the term or even the school year. Read them over and look at the marks you received. As you look at the writing with fresh eyes, do you agree with the marks and the comments? Why or why not?

Activity:
"Developing an argument"
pg. 79   (80 min.)

Purpose:
To help students write a formal essay.

The student activities unfold in a straightforward and logical manner. Introduce the activities with the opening of the first activity sheet. The discussion questions will review a few key concepts before students attempt to plan and develop their own essays based on the topic, "Endless TV channels but nothing to watch." The additional activity below suggests a plan for summing up the activity.

Discussion questions

What are the ways you could diagram your ideas?
How will you decide which ideas to keep and use?

Additional activity: In small groups, read your essays aloud to each other. Select a volunteer to read her or his essay to the whole class when the class group reconvenes. When all the volunteers have read their essays, decide whether or not you agree with the original statement, "Endless TV channels but nothing to watch."

Activity:
  "Evaluating an argument"
  pg. 81   (40 min.)

Purpose:
  To help students learn how to evaluate arguments.

Read aloud the article entitled "Delta Burke sparks a sizeable anger" and use the discussion questions to introduce the activities. The additional activity could be conducted in small group discussions with the small groups reporting back when the class group reconvenes or it could take the form of a brief written assignment.

Discussion questions

What kind of feelings did you experience as you listened to this article? What made you feel that way?
With what in the article, if anything, do you strongly disagree? Why?

Additional activity: Is there a gender difference in the way we view weights? Do men suffer the same kind of problems? Discuss the differences and similarities and the reasons behind the differences.

Activity:
  "Writing an argument"
  pg. 83   (80 min.)

Purpose:
  To provide students with additional practice in writing argumentative essays.

The first forty minutes are spent with the student partners planning the essay in detail. In the second forty minutes, the partners would split up and write their own versions of the essay. The discussion questions should be used when the pairs recombine to read each other's version of the jointly planned essay.

Discussion questions

How was your partner's version similar and different to your own essay? Since you planned the essay together, how do you account for the differences?

Additional activity: Decide which essay you would like to share with others. Reconvene in small groups or as a class and read essays aloud.

Activity:
  "Using a thesaurus"
  pg. 84   (80 min.)

Purpose:
  To help students learn how to use a thesaurus.

This activity requires each student to have a thesaurus to examine and use. Students generally prefer using an alphabetically arranged thesaurus. The discussion questions are meant to introduce the activities.

Discussion questions

What keeps you from using a thesaurus more often?
Is there such a problem as using a thesaurus too often?
How often do you think professional writers use a thesaurus?

Additional activity: Take out one of the early essays you composed. Put a check mark beside those words for which you would like to find a substitute. Use the thesaurus to find a better word. Read the revised essay to yourself. Did you make too many changes, too few, or just enough?

Activity:
  "Checklist for essay writing"
  pg. 87

Purpose:
  To provide students with a structure for checking their essays.

This activity is ongoing. Instruct students to include this checklist wherever they complete and collect their writing. Before handing in a piece for marking, they need to check off each point. You might consider having them hand in their checklist with each piece of writing to ensure they actually complete it, and to provide a focal point for student/teacher evaluation conferences.

Planning an essay

There are five main types of essays, and each needs a different style of writing:

1. **Story** (or narrative)
2. **Descriptive writing** in which you try to bring out the character and atmosphere of a place or scene
3. **Personal writing** in which you describe a true experience
4. **Argumentative** (or discursive) **writing** in which you analyze and discuss evidence and give your views on a subject such as "Should people have the right to decide when to end their own lives?"
5. **Factual writing/reporting**

There are four important stages to the writing of an essay: choosing a title, planning, writing, and checking.

Choosing a title

Look for the topic which you know something about and which interests you. The less you know about a subject the more ordinary your ideas will be.

Read the titles below then note beside each which type of essay is required. Some titles might be suited to more than one style of writing.

1. An afternoon in town.
2. The Dare.
3. "Television is a much more powerful force for good or evil than the printed word." Do you agree?
4. "Two pairs of eyes" — Imagine a setting or place observed from two contrasting viewpoints, such as a seaside resort as seen by a deck-chair attendant and a teenager, or a busy town centre as seen by a person with a disability and a taxi driver.
5. "On the Receiving End" — Describe a real or imaginary experience of unjust punishment.

Planning

This is particularly important for descriptive, factual and argumentative essays. This is the opportunity to plan your ideas, your examples and your time. Planning makes sure you don't repeat yourself or write something which is not relevant to the title.

A good way to plan is this: First find the chief idea of the essay and then jot down around it some of the most important points. You can then add examples if you wish. You might use a spray or pattern note to see the essay as a whole; to make links between the different sections of the essay and then to number the points in order of importance.

Example: Unemployed people should have to work to earn their benefits.

Try to see both sides of the question, but if you believe strongly in one side of the argument then argue for that. Always give reasons for your views.

Now plan an essay on this title: *What is wrong with our education?*

Beginning an essay

Remember that someone is going to read what you have written, so you should try to "hook" your reader.

Compare the following opening sentences of essays written on the title "The pressures on teenagers today are greater than they have ever been".

A. *There are many different views about this topic, and these differ according to the age and experience of the person answering.*

B. *The pressures on teenagers today are a lot worse than many years ago.*

C. *For various reasons most teenagers today are becoming part of a corrupt society.*

D. *As a national average, one of the most discomforting threats to teenagers, as a whole, is the subject of unemployment and its damaging properties.*

E. *The teenagers of today face a multitude of problems.*

Which are the best opening sentences? _____

Choose the least effective opening sentence. Write an improved version of it. _____

_____

_____

_____

_____

Compare these opening sentences for a descriptive essay set at the seaside.

A. *The golden sands were crowded by holiday makers as they stretched out in their bikinis to tan their pale bodies.*

B. *Stretching for miles is the empty, lifeless, rain-swept beach.*

C. *The car park was packed with people unloading picnics and children from their cars.*

D. *The sea, rough and deep, swirls insanely against the dark rocks.*

E. *The beach was deserted, the waves were angry and showed this by bashing themselves against the sea wall.*

F. *The sea thundered against the solid rock, as if willing it to collapse.*

Do any of these make you want to read on? _____

Why? _____

_____

_____

Now write your own opening sentence on this topic. _____

_____

_____

_____

Read carefully these opening sentences for a story called "Girl meets Boy".

A. *Sandra Dean is shy, but overall a delightful young lady.*

B. *The quick rhythm of the alarm clock blocked out the deep breathing of Mary O'Brien.*

C. *Umar, a young, good-looking, university student was on vacation for six weeks.*

D. *"Look everybody! Here comes Romeo."*
   "Romeo? Romeo? Where art thou Romeo?"
   They were all clapping and cheering as I approached them.

E. *Phil swung his worn leather satchel over his shoulder and let the door slam noisily behind him, not to the liking of the library assistants.*

Which of these opening sentences capture your interest? _____

_____

Choose one of the openings which you think could be improved and rewrite it here. _____

_____

_____

_____

_____

_____

_____

_____

_____

Tick the best opening for an essay entitled "How I have changed in the last twelve months."

A. *Twelve months ago I was still running around like an infant, enjoying myself and not attempting to work towards my future.*

B. *Last year, in grade 10, I obeyed the rules about wearing the school uniform, but this year my attitude has changed tremendously.*

C. *After ten years at school I finally discovered I could no longer get along with my teachers and I frequently found myself in the principal's office.*

D. *For the last twelve months of my life I have realized slowly how my life is beginning to change.*

E. *Twelve months ago I had the self confidence of a five-year-old on her first day at school.*

Now write your own opening sentence on this theme. _____

_____

_____

_____

Revising an essay

Read the following opening paragraphs written in answer to the question: "Why was the cotton industry so important in the Industrial Revolution?"

Which is better? _____

Why? _____

1. Between 1770 and 1825 the cotton industry revolutionized many aspects of life in England. Because of the cotton industry people stopped working at home and began working for someone else in a factory. Inventions powered by water or steam, such as the power loom, made it more profitable and quicker to make cotton goods in a factory. To help transport the raw cotton and the manufactured goods, canals and then railways were developed, especially in the northwest of England where the cotton industry was born.

2. The cotton industry was very important in the Industrial Revolution. Mainly it was important because it helped to improve railways in the country. Before the cotton industry became important the roads were in a poor condition. After the Industrial Revolution people and goods were able to move by railway. It was George Stephenson who invented railways powered by steam.

Presentation

If an essay looks well presented, in other words it is neat, clearly written and well paragraphed, then whoever is reading or marking it starts off with a favorable impression.

Checking

This is the quickest, and yet for most students the hardest, task. You need to check your essays for

1. Sentences that don't quite make sense.
2. Words left out.
3. Spelling mistakes.
4. Missing punctuation, especially quotation marks and question marks.
5. If you begin a story in the past tense you should not, without good reason, change to the present tense.
6. Consistency in your use of detail and names.
7. Consistency of viewpoint: if you begin a story in the third person ("She crept into the house . . .") do not change to the first person ("I closed the front door quietly behind me . . .").

If you are writing an important essay you may not be satisfied with your first version. You could then read this to a friend or member of your family. Ask them for their comments about your ideas and style. If you have no one who will listen to your work it is still a good idea to read it aloud to yourself. Often you will hear things which need to be improved, but which you didn't notice when reading the essay silently.

**In an exam it is a foolish waste of time to write an essay once
and then to copy it out again.**

Evaluating an essay

Read this essay about teenagers and parents which was written by a teenager.

Teenage life is one of the most hectic and confusing periods of your life. Conflict always arises between you and your parents. While you are trying to grow up, they are trying to keep you young.

Fathers cannot accept the fact that their "little girls" are growing up. Very soon some suitable young man will come along and take them away. When this happens it makes your dad feel old and neglected. He believes you are leaving him for another man, and in a way you are. He thinks you should be loyal, just like a wife. When fathers look at their daughters they probably see a carbon-copy of their wives when they were young.

On the other hand, mothers have the same attitude but a totally different motive. They can see their daughters maturing into elegant young ladies, like they once were. Could it be a hint of jealousy?

Obviously parents are afraid of losing you but they try to squeeze you into a jam-jar. It is as if you are being preserved. They believe that once you have stepped outside their door you disregard them and push them aside. But that isn't true.

Growing up isn't a disease that takes all your love away. If anything, you grow wiser and appreciate people more.

Parents think they are helping you but really they are making it worse. They are forcing responsibilities on you, but you cannot handle them all at once. This encourages young people to be defiant and just give up.

This is the time of your life when you need to make your own decisions. Parents try to imprint their own ideas on you. But you cannot be something that you really aren't. They have a future all worked out for you and they are insensitive and completely ignore your opinions and the way you feel. You have to discover for yourself that the world isn't as perfect as it seems to be. In their eyes you very often do not live up to their expectations but you learn by your mistakes.

Growing up is something that happens to everyone and no one can prevent it. Age is like a never-ending path with obstacles that you meet at some time or another.

By Alison Mather, age 15

1. Sum up each paragraph in one sentence.

2. Decide whether you

   a) agree or disagree with Alison's view in general and

   b) agree or disagree with Alison's views in your own case.

3. Discuss the essay with three or four other people.

4. What do you think Alison's parents are like?

5. How do you think Alison's parents might react if they read this?

6. A teacher who read the essay commented that, although it was interesting and realistic, the essay lacked specific examples from the writer's experience. Do you agree?

7. Write your own essay based on the title "Teenagers and parents."

8. What advice would you give to parents of teenagers?

9. Ask some parents to read the essay and record their comments and views.

Developing an argument

As your language skills develop, so will your ability to produce a quality piece of writing that explores the arguments and issues of any particular topic.

This style of writing demands both:

❏ well developed language skills

❏ a clear idea of how to plan and structure the content.

In expository and persuasive writing you should show these abilities:

At a **basic level**, the ability

❏ to express a point of view in a structured way

❏ to support a point of view by the use of evidence

❏ to recognize other points of view and to comment on these.

At a more **sophisticated level**, the ability

❏ to consider many aspects of an issue in a logical order

❏ to present a balanced view — points both for and against

❏ to use and evaluate evidence in order to form generalizations and conclusions

❏ to speculate on the wider implications of an argument.

How can we achieve this? Consider this model for planning:

An Expository Piece of Writing

Expository essays have a certain structure — a framework that helps us to organize our ideas.

1. They have an **Introductory Paragraph** that explains what the subject area is,

   ❏ how the title has been interpreted

   ❏ what the essay sets out to do — its aims.

2. The **main part of the essay** is a discussion of the issues. These need to be structured so that they are logically presented and balanced.

For	*Against*
1.	1.
2.	2.
3.	3.
4.	4.
5.	5.

These points need to be discussed in detail, using evidence, your own experience, analysis, and opinion. Explain your points fully and carefully.

3. The essay must be brought to a close with a **concluding paragraph**. After considering and analyzing pieces of evidence, draw various conclusions in your mind. Draft out what you feel to be your main conclusion(s).

Developing an argument 2

1. Use the topic, "*Endless TV channels but nothing to watch.*" Do you agree with this view of television?

   Work with a partner or small group. Produce below your own diagrammatic plan that helps you to collect your ideas and see the essay as a whole. Link these different points to form "parts" of your essay. Put these "parts" into an appropriate order for discussion.

2. Develop your ideas into the framework for the main body of the essay. Use subheadings and brief notes.

   _____

   _____

   _____

   _____

3. At this stage you are ready to draft your introduction — a paragraph or two. Remember! The introduction does not start to discuss the issues in detail. Its job is to set the scene.

   _____

   _____

   _____

   _____

4. Develop each heading from your framework into a paragraph. In factual writing, a paragraph should contain a key sentence which states its theme. This is often, but not always, at the beginning. Factual paragraphs also contain support sentences which add more information.

Evaluating an argument

As is evident in the following newspaper article, a "size 2" viewer was deeply offended by a television commercial for a line of clothes for "full-figured" women. She addresses her concerns to the promoter of the clothing line, an actress named Delta Burke, herself a "full-figured" woman. How much do you agree or disagree with the writer's arguments?

Delta Burke sparks a sizeable anger

I am absolutely furious with Delta Burke.

Her recent televised commercial where she floats into a boardroom with an entourage of big-boned women has me seething with rage. She very cheerfully goes about bashing slim women by comparing size 2, which I am, to the size of a finger puppet and then moves her hips, which are sizeable, and says that these clothes are for women with hips. Well it wasn't so very long ago that Delta was trying to rid herself of those very hips that she is praising. Now that she is pushing a line of clothes for bigger women, it is suddenly a good thing to have big hips and absolutely deplorable to be slim. Delta has failed in all of her attempts to become svelte so has decided to help other similar sized women by designing a line of clothes that will fit them and enlarge her pocketbook.

I am delighted that Delta has finally accepted her body for what it is and has stopped obsessing about being slim. I take issue, however, with the putdowns she makes about slim women. I'm sorry, Delta, but there's a part of me that believes there is residual bitterness and anger against slim women in what you've done. If there wasn't, there would be no mention about us in your commercial. You would be content to promote your clothes without attacking differently sized women.

This commercial is only one source of offensive comments made to and about slim women. We seem to be fair game for rude, insensitive remarks, and no one except thin women seem to understand this is a form of abuse. What would happen if Calista Flockhart, or another slim woman breezed into that same boardroom with a group of fine-boned, thin women and said her line of clothes was not for those heavies who are size 18 and certainly not for those with wide, flabby behinds. What a stink would be raised! There would be phone calls, E-mails and letters. The talk show hosts would rant and rave and say how awful that the heavy women of America were being persecuted and made fun of because of body size.

Well, I am making a stink. I am protesting, and not for the heavy people of the world, but for all of us thin women who have quietly accepted the insults, the put downs, the jokes and the rudeness. We are offended when we are referred to as skinny. We resent people asking how much we weigh, what size we wear, or if we have an eating disorder. We dislike the condescending attitude of the heavy people who tell us we are so lucky to be so thin. Are we really? Do you know how we really feel about weight? Do they know that some slim people have a problem keeping weight on regardless of how much they eat? Do they know that as teens we, too, were called names and were made to feel badly about our bodies? There are as many hurtful words used against thin people as there are against heavier people; the only difference is that society has made it acceptable to use these words against the slim. There is an unspoken message that we should be grateful that we are thin and as such should be able to take a little harmless ribbing now and then.

It is my belief that remarks made to people about their size crosses a boundary that should not be crossed. Because people do not react to comments about size does not mean they are not hurt by these words. I may have managed to survive all the comments about my ever-stable weight, but I am tired of being polite about it. I am tired of the tactlessness, and I am tired of the presumption that I do not have feelings. I do not starve myself; I do not have an eating disorder; I do wear size 2. It's nothing to be proud of; it's nothing to be ashamed of; it's just the way it is. And it is my business.

C.R. Macchiusi, Toronto Star

1. Read the paragraph beginning "Her recent televised commercial . . ." Write the key sentence that explains what the author claims Delta Burke is saying about bigger women and thin women.

_____

_____

2. Read the paragraph beginning "I am delighted that Delta . . ." Write the key sentence that the author offers as proof that Delta feels bitterness and anger towards thin women.

_____

_____

3. Read the paragraph beginning "This commercial is only one source . . ." How would you describe the kind of argument the author has made here? How convincing do you find this kind of argument? Explain.

_____

_____

_____

_____

4. Read the paragraph beginning "Well, I am making a stink." Make a list in point form of the problems the author claims thin people have. How would you say these problems compare to the problems overweight people have? Explain your position.

_____

_____

_____

_____

5. Read the article for the key words and phrases that reveal the author's emotional state and list them. Explain whether or not you feel this kind of emotion was justified and why you think this way.

_____

_____

_____

_____

6. The article is entitled "Delta Burke sparks a sizeable anger." Explain why you think this title was chosen and why you think it is either effective or ineffective.

_____

_____

_____

_____

Writing an argument

Work with a partner. Select one of the titles below and complete the framework.

1. How should children be brought up?

2. "A woman has to do twice as well as a man in order to be thought half as good." (Charlotte Woolf). Is this still true?

3. "Being a teenager today is more difficult than in our parents' days." Discuss this opinion, in the light of your experience.

4. What is wrong with the educational system?

5. "Tobacco and alcohol companies should have no part to play in the sponsorship of sporting activities." Do you agree?

6. Should experiments on animals be permitted?

TITLE:_____

1. **Introduction**: Notes to include.

2. **Points for discussion**: subheadings.

3. **Conclusions**: Notes to include.

Using a thesaurus

For instant extension . . . . use the thesaurus

"Proper words in proper places, make the true definition of a style" Jonathan Swift 1720

A vital aspect of every piece of written work is the quality of the vocabulary that you select to express your ideas. In particular, redrafting your work offers opportunities for improving the quality of the vocabulary.

A student's ability to pluck exactly the right word out of the air may be . . .

good   able, accomplished, capable, clever, conscientious, creditable, efficient, excellent, fabulous, gifted, lovely, pleasing, proficient, skilful, skilled, talented, terrific.

bad   appalling, awful, calamitous, dire, dreadful, frightful, ghastly, hair-raising, hideous, horrible, nasty, severe, shocking, terrible, unfortunate, unpleasant.

or

indifferent   commonplace, fair, mediocre, middling, moderate, ordinary, unexciting, uninteresting.

The thesaurus is designed to help us all

❏ make good use of the words we already know

❏ add to the range of our vocabulary

❏ improve our knowledge and understanding of language generally.

There are a number of different thesauri available.
Each student should select the appropriate one and learn how to use it.

The Education System

A group of students have been planning a discursive assignment about "What is wrong with the education system?" Sarah has recorded their comments so that she could draft them into her essay.

Too many lessons are boring. They are all alike. There's too much listening to teachers who talk too much, making lots of notes that you will never need.

Teachers forget how to make lessons good.

Learning should be fun.

Some topics are rubbish.

They should point out the relevance of the topics. I mean sometimes we can't see the forest for the trees. It's not enough — not for me anyway — to say it's on the exam.

Teachers have too many rules that are pathetic.

I learn best from teachers who treat me as an individual.

A. Sarah recognized that while the ideas were useful, she needed to re-think some of the wording. Sarah turned to her thesaurus and constructed a list. Complete the list.

Word used	*Alternatives to consider*
boring	dreary, dull, long-winded, monotonous, tedious, uninteresting
alike	akin, analogous, identical, matching, resembling, similar
need	depend on, desire, have occasion for, require, want
make	_____ _____
good	_____ _____
fun	_____ _____
rubbish	_____ _____
pathetic	_____ _____

B. Redraft the group's ideas into a paragraph that reads fluently and uses more sophisticated vocabulary.

_____

_____

_____

_____

_____

_____

_____

_____

_____

C. Working as a small group add another paragraph of your own.

❏ collect the ideas on paper.

❏ reconsider your choice of words using a thesaurus to help you.

❏ redraft the ideas into a paragraph.

_____

_____

_____

_____

_____

_____

_____

_____

_____

D. Select an assignment that you are working on at the moment.

❏ Read it through carefully. In particular see if anything could be phrased better.

❏ Use a thesaurus to consider whether an alternative word can express your ideas more closely, or capture the atmosphere more succinctly.

❏ Discuss the possible changes with a partner.

❏ Redraft the piece.

Checklist for essay writing

Summary

There are four vital stages in the writing of essays:

A. Choosing a title
B. Planning
C. Writing
D. Checking

Look at the checklist below before you begin. Then write your essay title on the right and check off the points before handing in your work.

Essay titles

1.	Is what I have written relevant to the title?					
2.	Have I written enough?					
3.	Have I avoided my previous mistakes?					
4.	Is each major idea developed in a separate paragraph?					
5.	Is there a logical development and conclusion to the essay?					
6.	Have I avoided clichés? (e.g. as quiet as a mouse)					
7.	Have I checked carefully for misspellings?					
8.	Have l checked carefully for words left out?					
9.	Have I checked carefully for the proper use of capital letters?					
10.	Have I checked carefully for the proper use of punctuation, speech, and question marks?					
11.	Have I kept a copy?					
For personal writing and stories						
12.	Have I included lively descriptions?					
13.	Have I used comparisons?					
14.	Have I varied the verbs of speech? (she shouted; he mumbled; she repeated menacingly)					

Unit 7

Exams

Tests and exams are too often perceived by students as isolated events in time; when they're over, they're over and there's not much anyone can do about a poor result. Meanwhile the opposite is true. Tests and exams actually are recurrent processes. Students need to learn how to manage their time and efforts in the period leading up to the test or exam, apply discrete skills to help unlock the test or exam paper itself, and reflect constructively afterwards on how best to improve the process next time around.

Activity:
"No surprises"
pg. 91 (40 min.)

Purpose:
To help students objectively assess their exam preparations.

Exams, term tests, unit quizzes: whatever they're called they strike terror into students' hearts. After they get their exam results, of course, students fervently make all sorts of resolutions about their approaches to the next set of exams; as time wears on, unfortunately, those resolutions take a back seat to more immediate concerns. This activity helps students reflect objectively on what they've achieved, what they hope to achieve, and what they're actually doing to achieve their goals. The activity will have the most impact about two weeks before a major set of exams. The discussion questions lead into the activity.

Discussion questions

What kind of study routines do you adopt before a new set of exams?
What kind of changes have you made in how you study since your last set of exams?
What makes you believe that your marks will change for the better this time around?

Additional activity: Make up a time management schedule that starts tomorrow and carries through until the exams. Mark down what you plan to study each day, when and for how long, and the approach you plan to use. Review your plan each day to assess how well you've achieved your study goals.

Activity:
"Writing exams" pg. 92
20 min.)

"Checking the exam paper"
pg. 93 (20 min.)

Purpose:
To review how best to manage exam questions.

These two activities deal with the nitty-gritty of handling an exam paper. As you guide them through the various sections, instruct students to place a check mark beside the points they feel are especially useful for them, or points they ordinarily forget in the heat of the moment. The additional activity reinforces those choices. As you move through the various points, you can adapt or elaborate on the advice to better suit the type of exam expected. The discussion questions introduce the activity.

Discussion questions

What's the difference on an exam between "comparing" and "contrasting?"
What's the difference between "justifying" and "discussing?"

Additional activity: Make your own list of point form reminders about the exam hints you ordinarily forget. Review that list just before an exam.

Activity:
"Exam dos and don'ts"
pg. 94   (40 min.)

Purpose:
To offer students practical suggestions in preparation for an upcoming exam.

As students read through the article, ask them to check the suggestions they think they might profitably adopt. The additional activity instructs them in how to apply those suggestions. The discussion questions sum up their reflections, and ask them to elaborate on the advice in the article.

Discussion questions

What suggestions mentioned in the article for exam preparation have worked for you?
What suggestions *not* mentioned in the article do you think might work for other people?

Additional activity: Review the suggestions that you would like to incorporate into your own exam preparations. Put these suggestions into point form in your own language and post them in the room you intend to use for studying.

Activity:
"Self-assessment 1: Keeping track"
pg. 95   (20 min.)

"Self-assessment 2: Progress report"
pg. 96   (20 min.)

Purpose:
To help students monitor their progress.

Photocopy one of the "Self-assessment 1: Keeping track" sheets for each subject students need to track. Another approach would be for students to choose the one subject in which they most need to improve and track just that subject. During this activity, students can review the work that's been marked in this subject and list the results in chronological order. They can add a comment of their own elaborating on why they received the mark or evaluation and how satisfied they were with the results. The additional activity asks them to interpret this information. The discussion questions lead into the activity.

The second self-assessment sheet focuses on exam results and the related activities are self-explanatory and straightforward.

Discussion questions

How do you keep track of the marks and comments you receive on the work you do in each subject?
If you had a chronological list of marks and comments, of what use would it be to you?

Additional activity: Review the information from the chart you've produced and answer the following questions:
- What kind of work produces your best marks?
- What kind of work requires improvement?
- What kind of teacher comment has been made several times?
- After reviewing this information, what course of action can you take to improve your progress?

Activity:
"Handling stress"
pg. 97   (80 min.)

Purpose:
To help students handle the stress in their lives.

Emphasize in these activities that what might be stressful for one person might not be for another. Moreover, the kinds of stress students feel may not be obvious to adults. Any of the writing assignments should be treated as personal writing and privileged. If students make unexpected and serious disclosures, get advice from your guidance counsellor or administration on the appropriate course of action. The discussion questions lead into the activity.

Discussion questions

What kinds of situations generally cause people stress?
What do most adults *not* understand about the stress in a student's life?

Additional activity: Make a resolution about some action, big or small, that you plan on taking tomorrow. Write it down: "Tomorrow, I am going to . . ." When you take the action, tear up your resolution and throw it away. If you don't take the action, write another resolution and put it with the first one. When you take the action, tear them both up and throw them away.

Activity:
"Relaxation"
pg. 99   (40 min.)

Purpose:
To help students find ways to relieve their stress.

Students live stressful lives. They need to make relaxation an essential component of what they do every day. The discussion questions lead into this activity. The additional activity instructs students to be proactive in planning more relaxation time for themselves.

Discussion questions

What percentage of your weekday time is devoted to relaxing activities?
What percentage of your weekend time is devoted to relaxing activities?

Additional activity: Review what you do for relaxation and how often you're able to enjoy those activities. Write down the next seven days in a column. For each day, note in blue what you do for relaxation. If you don't have a relaxation activity for a particular day or need additional time, note something you can do about it in red pen. At the end of the seven days, review your progress toward daily relaxation and make a plan for the next seven days.

No surprises

Complete all sections **except for section D** before your next set of exams. Section D should be completed when all your exams have been returned.

A. List your subjects	B. Mark last report (or last year)	C. Mark you think you'll get	D. Mark you got
_____	_____	_____	_____
_____	_____	_____	_____
_____	_____	_____	_____
_____	_____	_____	_____
_____	_____	_____	_____
_____	_____	_____	_____
_____	_____	_____	_____
_____	_____	_____	_____
_____	_____	_____	_____
_____	_____	_____	_____

E. What is your best subject? _____

Why do you do well in this subject? _____

_____

_____

F. What subject gives you the most difficulty? _____

Why? _____

_____

_____

G. What steps are you taking in what subjects to ensure your exam results will improve over last term? If you haven't taken any steps yet, what can you do, starting today?

_____

_____

_____

_____

_____

_____

Writing exams

Keywords explained

Compare: Are the things very alike (similar) or are there important differences? Which do you think is best? Why?

Contrast: Look for differences.

Criticize: Use evidence to support your opinion on the value or merit of theories, facts, or views of others.

Define: Give the meaning.

Describe: Write in detail.

Differentiate: Explain the difference.

Discuss: Write about the important aspects of the topic, are there two sides to the question? Consider the arguments for and against.

Distinguish: Explain the difference.

Evaluate: Judge the importance or success.

Explain: Make clear.

Illustrate: Give examples which make the point clear.

Interpret: Explain the meaning in your own words, for example you may be asked to interpret a graph.

Justify: Give reasons to support an argument or action.

Outline: Choose the most important aspects of a topic. Ignore the minor detail.

Relate: Show the connection between things.

State: Write briefly the main points.

Summarize: Bring together the main points.

Trace: Show how something has developed from beginning to end.

Key stages in answering exam questions.

1. Scan all the questions.

2. Mark all the questions you could answer.

3. Read these questions carefully.

4. Choose the correct number (in each section).

5. Decide on an order: best answers first.

6. Divide up your time.

7. Underline key words in the question.

8. Plan your answer.

9. **Stick to the point of the question.**

10. Write your answer.

11. Use the plan at every stage e.g. every paragraph.

12. Check your answer against the plan. Watch for mistakes.

13. If you have time, re-read all your answers and make any necessary corrections.

Checking the exam paper

The question paper is yours. Make full use of it to:

(a) Note down things that occur to you as you read it
(b) Mark which questions you intend to do
(c) Underline key words in questions
(d) Plan answers.

Note down the times you should complete each section.
A 1:30-2:00
B 2:00-3:00
C 3:00-4:00

Friday 27 June, 1:30-4:00, 2½ hours.

Careless and untidy work will be penalized.

The total time for the three sections in this paper is 2½ hours. You should spend about half an hour on section A, about an hour on section B, and an hour on section C.

Answer all questions in section A and two in each of sections B and C.

20% of marks are awarded in section A.
40% of marks in section B.
40% of marks in section C.

Take note of the number of marks for each section. More time is needed on questions that have the most marks.

Answer the 20 questions in section A on the grid provided. One mark is given for each correct answer. Marks are not deducted for wrong answers.

Make sure **you know** where to write your answers.

Mark them clearly. Sometimes your ideas become clearer towards the end of an exam.

Read each section carefully, come back to any questions you find too difficult.

There are different groups of questions in this section. Instructions are given at the beginning of each group.

These are multiple choice questions. If you do not know the right answer, eliminate any that are definitely wrong.

For each question there are five possible answers. When you have chosen the alternative which you think to be the best answer to a question, mark it on the answer sheet. Use an HB pencil to mark your answers in the same way as in the example. Rub out your answer if you change your mind. DO NOT USE A PEN.

These are provided by your school.

Use the answer book provided to give your answers to questions in sections B and C. Do not use the answer book for rough work. Use the question sheet.

You will usually have to provide your own. Even when you use a calculator the exam may require you to show the stages of your working out.

Mathematical tables are needed.

You are allowed to use calculators.

Sometimes important data is provided here, e.g. in a physics exam:
Acceleration of free fall (due to gravity), g, = 9 81 ms^{-2}

Exam dos and don'ts

Some tips for handling the stress

More and more, it seems, the future hangs on examination results and hardly anybody can now escape being judged on what can be remembered and reproduced in a few hours of writing and writhing.

The build-up to important exams is, for many, punctuated by periods of intense anxiety and stress, panic that not enough work has been done, fears that results may not be good enough to take one to the next stage — and possibly yet more exams.

Although a certain amount of keyed-upness may be necessary to bring out the best, stress and anxiety are counter-productive.

Dr. David Lewis, a clinical psychologist, who holds regular de-stressing workshops for examination candidates, says: "A great fear of examinations seems to be built into us from an early age. You have to bear in mind that there is nothing you cannot achieve, that you need only ordinary intelligence levels to pass most exams, and that if you build up confidence through adequate preparation, there is simply nothing to fear."

It is even possible to avoid exam stress and enjoy the challenge, buzz, and sense of achievement that exams can bring, by bearing in mind these essential examination dos and don'ts:

❏ Remember that you can actually decide to succeed — and that everything follows from that.

❏ Bear in mind that stress can be catching, and can be worked up deliberately, so don't moan constantly to friends about how much work you haven't done or listen to people who tell you they can't sleep, or are sick with worry. Reassure each other instead.

❏ Realize that we all have a limited concentration span, and that even the world's greatest geniuses will start flagging after an hour and a half, at most. Take short breaks every hour or so for 10 minutes, then you'll start studying with renewed energy.

❏ Don't drink lots of strong coffee. Caffeine encourages adrenaline production, which in turn increases anxiety. One or two cups a day is enough. Otherwise drink herbal teas, fruit juice, or mineral water.

❏ Don't shun absolutely all delights to live laborious days. The occasional party, or social evening does no harm (so long as it's not the night before an important exam) and can even contribute to concentration the next day. Reward yourself with leisure activities and interests, particularly after a hard session of studying.

❏ Relax and unwind before going to bed by listening to a relaxation tape, soothing music, or by watching a relaxation video. Do not attempt to relax by watching a horror movie late at night — this will increase stress the next morning and may prevent sleep.

❏ If you have difficulty sleeping, practise simple yoga techniques, or place a softer pillow under your usual one. A good night's sleep wards off anxiety and reduces stress next morning.

❏ Although intense studying the night before the exam is a bad idea, glancing through notes just before you go to bed helps to imprint the subject on the memory.

❏ Do not attempt, at this late stage, to learn any facts you don't understand. You'll never be able to recall them properly.

❏ When writing an exam, don't worry if time runs out during essay papers. Writing notes, rather than fully rounded sentences, can clock up a surprising amount of marks. Also, remember that thoughts often flow during the writing of exams — it's not always necessary to plan every single thing before writing.

❏ Whatever you do, never indulge in detailed post-mortems after each exam. It's over — forget it. Post-mortems induce anxiety and achieve nothing.

❏ Most important of all, believe in yourself. Believe that you can do well in these exams. Don't fall prey to negative self-fulfilling prophecies, or tell yourself that you are no good at exams. They're not a test of your worth as a human being, just an indication of your current level of expertise in a subject.

❏ Even if you do fail, all is not lost. Most exams can be retaken these days, and the will to succeed is always more important than any perceived ability or inability in any subject. Remember that most exam failures are caused by lack of self-confidence rather than lack of intelligence or learning ability.

Self-assessment 1: Keeping track

For assignments, projects, essays, and all marked work **Subject** _____

❏ Check your progress   ❏ Improve your standards   ❏ Learn from your mistakes

DATE	TITLE OF WORK	MARK/TEACHER COMMENT	MY COMMENT

Self assessment 2: Progress report

Rate your own progress by writing this report on yourself. Be honest and realistic.

Quality of Work Grades

A. Much better understanding than previously

B. Getting more confident; generally better understanding

C. Problems seem to arise just as frequently; I do well in some aspects

D. I'm having trouble keeping up

E. I don't understand this subject

Effort Grades

1. Working very hard

2. Working hard

3. Making a fair effort

4. Not quite enough time or trouble taken

5. I need to start working now

Subject	Exam Date	Quality	Effort	Action needed

Action plans:

For each item in the "Action needed" column, set out a detailed action plan. Indicate what you are going to do, which days and at what time you will take that action, how long you plan to continue, and how you will evaluate the effectiveness of your plan.

Handling stress

"I feel trapped. There is no way out. The walls are closing in on me. There is no door. I shout for help. No one answers. There is pressure on my chest. My heart is pounding. It seems as if it will burst. My head feels like it's in a vice."

Stress and Pressure

There is a difference between *stress* and *pressure*. Stress can be like a nightmare. It can stop you from doing things. Pressure can provide a way of urging you into new and interesting things. Without pressure life could be very tedious. The secret is for you to be in control of the pressure and not allow it to become stressful.

Understanding Stress

Make a list of events which have left you feeling stressed. Explain these events to a partner.

How did you handle the stress at the time?

How do you think you should have handled it?

Could you have avoided the stress? How?

Remember that individuals differ an enormous amount in what they find stressful.

Ways of Feeling Less Stressed

1. **Talk to Someone** *A problem shared is a problem halved.*

   Who would you go to for help in these circumstances:
   ❏ when work is overwhelming?
   ❏ when you are feeling unable to cope with a personal problem?

   Think of someone in school or at home who:
   ❏ can always be relied on.
   ❏ is going to cheer you up.
   ❏ is going to be honest with you.
   ❏ will listen to you.

   Think, write, or talk about a time when you have turned to someone for help. What happened?

2. **Feel Healthy**
   Do you know what your body needs?

   Think about these points:
   Do you get enough sleep?

   Do you eat regularly and have breakfast every day?

   Are you eating a healthy, varied diet?

   Do you take regular exercise?

Are you about the right weight for your height?

Do you smoke?

Do you do relaxation exercises?

Discuss these points with a close friend, and write a report that describes yourself in ten sentences.

_____

_____

_____

_____

_____

_____

_____

_____

It is very difficult to break **bad habits** which are long established. Smokers, for example, know the harm that cigarettes are doing to them, but they blot this out and convince themselves it doesn't apply to them.

❏ The first stage is to admit to yourself there's a problem.
❏ The second stage is to decide on the best course of action.

If you aren't really committed to making a change, you won't succeed.

3. **Manage your time**

Look at how you manage your time. If you leave things to the last minute and then panic, ask yourself how you could start to change this habit.

Rewards: If you feel you can improve things, write down what you are going to do. Then write the reward you'll give yourself if you keep to the promise. Pin the piece of paper somewhere prominently at home.

4. **Be assertive — Stick up for yourself!**

❏   Learn to say no if that's what would be best in a particular situation.
❏   Sometimes you just have to say no to stop yourself being overloaded.
❏   Get things clear before you commit yourself to something.

Practise:

Role play: you have a lot of work to do and a friend wants to come for the evening for help with homework.

Role play: a friend wants you to watch a video when you really should be doing some school work.

Relaxation

There are many successful ways to relax and rid yourself of stress. Look for a way that works for you. Here are a few suggestions:

Swimming, which is one of the most relaxing of all sports.

A quick way (30 seconds to a minute) to relax is to stand up straight, stretch up, bend forward, then let your head and arms hang down while keeping your legs straight.

Yoga is a wonderful way to relieve tension. Try joining a group in your area and go once or twice a week.

Have an absorbing hobby such as reading, listening to music, watching a film. There are as many ways of unwinding as there are people.

List possible ways of relaxing and note beside each whether you sometimes, often, or never do these things.

Possible ways of relaxing	Sometimes	Often	Never

Index

Abbreviations, 17, 24
Aboriginal folk tale, 44–45
Achievers and underachievers, 61, 68
Activities
    Abbreviations, 17, 24
    Achievers and underachievers, 61, 68
    Additional, 6, 7, 8, 16, 17, 25, 26, 27, 38, 39, 40, 60,
        61, 62, 70, 71, 72, 88, 89, 90
    Alternate ways to make notes, 17, 22, 23
    Analyze work and study habits, 6, 9
    Analyze types of note making, 16, 18, 19
    Assess exam preparations, 88, 91
    Begin an essay, 70, 74–76
    Bibliographies and references, 27, 37
    Check the exam paper, 88, 93
    Checklist for essay writing, 72, 87
    Computer research, 27, 35–36
    Concentration and motivation, 61, 66
    Develop an argument, 71, 79–80
    Effective note making, 16, 19
    Evaluate an argument, 72, 81–82
    Evaluate an essay, 71, 78
    Evaluate time management, 7, 12
    Evaluate your study environment, 8, 15
    Handle stress, 90, 97–98
    Identify learning roadblocks, 60, 65
    Improve yourself, 61, 68
    Independent study or research projects, 26, 32–34
    Ineffective note making, 16, 18
    Interpret data, 40, 50–52
    Key words in note making, 17, 21
    Manage exam questions, 88, 92, 93
    Map use of time, 7, 11
    Match reading material and purpose, 38, 41
    Memorization, 60, 63, 64
    Memory tricks, 60, 64
    Monitor progress, 89, 95, 96
    Pattern notes, 17, 23
    Pinpoint your problems, 61, 67
    Plan an essay, 70, 73
    Plan your time, 8, 13, 14
    Practise reading strategies, 39, 44–46
    Practise skimming and scanning, 38, 42, 43
    Prepare for exams, 89, 94
    Present data, 40, 53
    Rate your notes, 16, 20
    Recommended reading, 40, 54–59
    Reflect on learning, 62, 69
    Relaxation, 90, 99
    Revise an essay, 71, 77
    Search for books, 26, 31
    Select the right book, 25–26, 30
    Self-assessment, 89, 95, 96
    Set goals, 6, 10
    Sprays, 17, 22
    SQ3R, 39, 47–48
    Understand memory, 60, 63
    Unlock new vocabulary, 39, 49
    Use a thesaurus, 72, 84–86
    Use the library efficiently, 25, 28–29
    Write an argument, 72, 83
    Write an exam, 88, 92
Alaska, 43
Alternate ways of making notes, 17, 22, 23
Analyzing types of note making, 16, 18, 19
Animal Farm, 54, 57
Antarctica, 43
Arawak, 47, 48
Arctic, 43
Argument
    Developing, 71, 79–80
    Evaluating, 72, 81–82
    Writing, 72, 83
Aria, 29
Arteries, 18, 19
Assessing exam preparations, 88, 91
Atom, 66
Atrium, 18, 19
Average hours spent watching TV, 52
Average price of a gallon of gas, 53
Avery, Valerie, 55, 59
Awake and Dreaming, 55, 58

Badger on the Barge, 54, 56
Bar graph, 52
Beginning an essay, 70, 74–76
Bell, William, 54, 56
Bering Strait, 43
Beyond the Chocolate War, 54, 56
Bibliographies, 27, 37
Black holes, 29
Blood, 18, 19
Book, Rick, 54, 56
Bois, Y.A., 37
Bova, Ben, 54, 56
Brooks, Martha, 54, 56
Brother in the Land, 55, 58
Brown, Dee, 47, 48
Burke, Delta, 72, 81, 82
Bury My Heart at Wounded Knee, 47, 48

Bury the Dead, 54, 56
Byron, Lord, 29

Cal, 54, 57
Capillaries, 18, 19
Carter, Peter, 54, 56
The Catcher in the Rye, 54, 57
CD-ROMs, 25, 33, 35, 36, 37
Checking exam papers, 88, 93
Checklist for essay writing, 72, 87
Children of the Dust, 54, 57
Chilterns, 43
Chinese proverbs, 69
The Chocolate War, 54, 56
Christian, 24
Cleveland, Grover, 21
Clinton, Bill, 21
The Clodhopper's Halloween Ball, 56
Columbus, Christopher, 47, 48
Computer research, 27, 35–36
Concentration and motivation, 61, 66
Cook, Captain James, 21
Cormier, Peter, 54, 56
Coto Danana, 46
Cotswolds, 43
Cotton fibres, 45

Developing an argument, 71, 79–80
Dewey classification codes, 28, 33
Dickinson, Peter, 54, 56
Discussion questions, 6, 7, 8, 16, 17, 25, 26, 27, 38, 39,
    40, 60, 61, 62, 70, 71, 72, 88, 89, 90
Downs, 43
Doyle, Brian, 55, 58
Druids, 29
The Duelling Machine, 54, 56
Dunant, Henri, 24
Durrell, Gerald, 55, 59
Dust, 55, 58

Effective note making, 16, 19
E-mail, 17
Energy transfer, 42
England, 43
The Ennead, 54, 57
Epictetus, 69
Essays,
    Beginning, 70, 74–76
    Checklist, 72, 87
    Evaluating, 71, 78
    Expository, 79
    Planning, 70, 73
    Revising, 71, 77
    Writing, 70–87

Euripedes, 69
Eva, 54, 56
Evaluating an argument, 72, 81–82
Evaluating an essay, 71, 78
Evaluating time management, 7, 10, 12
Evaluating your study environment, 8, 15
Exams, 5, 7, 88–99
    Checking, 88, 93
    Preparing for, 89, 94
    Writing, 88, 92

Filene, E.A., 69
First aid, 23
Flockhart, Calista, 81
Fossil fuels, 45

Galloway, Priscilla, 55, 59
The Game, 56
Geneva Convention, 24
Goethe, 29
Goodnight Mr. Tom, 54, 57
Greenland, 43

Handling stress, 90, 97–98
Hautzig, Deborah, 55, 58
Hawaii, 21
Hawaiian Monarchy, 17, 21
Heart, 18, 19
Heraclitus, 69
Hero of Lesser Causes, 55, 58
Hershey, John, 55, 59
Hiroshima, 55, 59
Ho, Minfong, 54, 56
Hold Fast, 54, 57
Homecoming, 54, 57
Honolulu, 21
Howker, Janni, 54, 56

Identifying learning roadblocks, 60, 65
If I Just Had Two Wings, 55, 58
Igneous rocks, 22
Improving work and study habits, 6
Improving yourself, 61, 68
Improving your note making, 16, 20
Independent study or research projects, 26, 32–34
Indicators of social development, 50
Industrial Revolution, 77
Ineffective note making, 16, 18
Internet, 25, 27, 35, 36
Interpreting data, 40, 50–52
Iolani Palace, 21
It's My Life, 55, 58

Jamestown, 48

Jerome, Jerome K., 69
Johnston, Julie, 55, 58

Kaiulani, Princess, 21
Kamehameha, 21
Kaufman, Bel, 69
Key words in note making, 17, 21
Knowles, John, 54, 56

Lava, 22
Lawrence, Louise, 54, 57
Learning, 60–69
Leeson, Robert, 55, 58
Library and research skills, 25–37
Liliuokalani, Queen, 21
Line graph, 52, 65
London Morning, 55, 59
Lorimer, James Horace, 69

MacLaverty, Bernard, 54, 57
The Maestro, 54, 56
Magma, 22
Magorian, Michelle, 54, 57
Major, Kevin, 54, 57
Making notes, 16–24
Managing exam questions, 88, 92, 93
Managing time and space, 6–15
Mapping your time, 7, 11
Marital status of persons 15 years and over, 51
Mark, Jan, 54, 57
Matching reading material and purpose, 38, 41
Matisse, 37
Matisse and Picasso, 37
Matthiessen, Paul, 55, 59
McKinley, William, 21
Mehta, Ved, 55, 59
A Memory of Solferino, 24
Memorization, 16, 60, 63, 64
Memory Tricks, 60, 64
Mendips, 43
Mnemonics, 60, 61, 64
Monet, 29
Monitoring progress, 89, 95, 96
Mt. Etna, 22
Muslim, 24
My Family And Other Animals, 55, 59

Necking with Louise, 54, 56
Needle, Jan, 54, 57
Nell's Quilt, 54, 57
News as a percent of TV programming, 52
Note making, 16–24
    Alternate methods, 17, 22, 23
    Effective, 16, 19

Ineffective, 16, 18
Improving, 16, 20
Key words, 17, 21
Rating, 16, 20
Nuclear power, 33, 45

Oberman, Sheldon, 55, 59
One Day in the Life of Ivan Denisovitch, 54, 57
Opening sentences, 70, 74–76
Orwell, George, 54, 57

Panama Canal, 43
Paris: Walking Tour of the Artist's Life in the City, 37
Pattern notes, 17, 23
Pearson, Kit, 55, 58
Pele, 21
Periodic table, 43
Picasso, Pablo, 37
Picasso: 200 Masterpieces from 1989–1972, 37
Pie graph, 51
Piggy in the Middle, 54, 57
Pinpointing your problems, 61, 67
Plagiarism, 35
Planning an essay, 60, 73
Planning your time, 8, 13, 14
Plasma, 18, 19
Platelets, 18, 19
Plato, 69
Pompeii, 22
Population for selected states, 53
Population projections for Canada, 53
Powhatans, 48
Practising reading strategies, 39, 44–46
Practising skimming and scanning, 38, 42, 43
Prefix, 39, 49
Preparing for exams, 89, 94
Presenting data, 40, 53
Princess Kaiulani, 21
Projects,
    Research and independent study, 5
A Proper Little Nooryeff, 55, 58
Publilius Syrus, 69

Queen Liliuokalani, 21
Questionnaire, 6, 9

Rating your notes, 16, 20
Reading strategies, 38–59
    Practice, 39, 44–46
Recommended reading, 40, 54–59
Red cells, 18, 19
Red Crescent, 24
Red Cross, 24
References, 27, 37

Reflecting on learning, 62, 69
Relaxation, 90, 99
Research and independent study projects, 5
Revising an essay, 71, 77
Rhue, Morton, 54, 57
Rice Without Rain, 54, 56
The River, 56

Salinger, J.D., 54, 57
San Salvador, 48
Saying Goodbye to the Tall Man, 56
Scanning, 38, 43
The Scarecrows, 54, 57
Schwartz, Virginia Frances, 55, 58
Searching for books, 26, 31
Second Star to the Right, 55, 58
Selecting the right book, 25–26, 30
Self-assessment, 89, 95, 96
A Separate Peace, 54, 56
Setting goals, 6, 10
The Shaman's Nephew, 55, 59
Skills,
    Library and research, 25–37
Skimming, 38, 42
Slade, Arthur, 55, 58
The Snow Leopard, 55, 59
Socrates, 29
Solferino, 24
Solzhenitsyn, Alexander, 54, 57
Sources of revenue for U.S. schools, 52
Sprays, 17, 22
SQ3R, 39, 47–48
Stones, 54, 56
Strategies,
    Reading, 38–59
    Research and independent study, 5
    Tests and examinations, 5
Study environment, 8, 15
Study week planner, 11, 14
Suez Canal, 43
Suffix, 39, 49
Sundogs, 56
Swift, Jonathan, 84
Swindells, Robert, 55, 58

Table, 50, 53
Taino, 47, 48

Talking in Whispers, 54, 57
Terris, Susan, 54, 57
Tests, 5
Thesaurus, 72, 84–86
Thoreau, Henry, 69
Three Men in a Boat, 69
Time management, 7, 8, 10, 12, 13, 14, 88
Tookoome, Simon, 55, 59
Too Young to Fight, 55, 59
True Confessions of a Heartless Girl, 54, 56
Tyrannosaurus, 29

Uncle Ronald, 55, 58
Understanding memory, 60, 63
The Undertaker's Gone Bananas, 55, 58
Unlocking new vocabulary, 39, 47
Ure, Jean, 55, 58
U.S. Congress, 21
U.S. Marines, 21
Using a thesaurus, 72, 84–86
Using key words in note making, 17, 21
Using the library efficiently, 25, 28–29
USSR, 43

Vedi, 55, 59
Vegetarian food, 46
Veins, 18, 19
Ventricles, 18, 19
Voigt, Cynthia, 54, 57
Volcanoes, 22

Wahunsonacook, 48
Watson, James, 54, 57
The Wave, 54, 57
Westall, Robert, 54, 57
White cells, 18, 19
Williams, E., 37
Woolf, Charlotte, 83
Work and study habits, 6, 9, 60
Writing an argument, 72, 83
Writing essays, 70–87
Writing exams, 88, 92
Wynne-Jones, Tim, 54, 56

Zindell, Paul, 55, 58